GRANDFATHER OF THE NICU

A PARENT'S JOURNEY

Vonstone Wolfe

ISBN 978-1-64300-260-6 (Paperback)
ISBN 978-1-64300-261-3 (Digital)

Covenant Books, Inc.
11661 Hwy 707
Murrells Inlet, SC 29576
www.covenantbooks.com

To the heroes of this narrative, Loretta and Joshua,
for their courage, strength, and inspiration to which
I only bore silent and adoring witness.

Before you were conceived, I wanted you. Before you
were born, I loved you. Before you were here an hour,
I would die for you. This is the miracle of love.

—Maureen Hawkins

CONTENTS

PROLOGUE

We've all got places to go, places we need to be, in our day-to-day lives. Sometimes, when we get there, we are greeted by others whom are also strangers to that place. On rare occasions, we come into contact with that person whom is veteran to the environment, someone who can—for all intents and purposes—show us the ropes or at the very least provide a friendly face, an amiable point of reference to steady us. As most are able to attest, new situations can be most daunting—that first day in a new school, the first day of sleep-away camp, or starting a new job—all new situations where there isn't likely to be found that proverbial friendly face. Most adults can attest, for most if not all, have experienced the discomfort felt when plunged into any of the aforementioned new situations. Of course, it does get easier after you've made that first friend; that lunch buddy, the one you sit next to on the bus, or meet up with after school.

No one now living, or I dare say who ever lived, can draw from their remembrance, what it was like to come into the world alone; that is, of course, except for those of us whom were born alone. Single birth is, without a doubt, the most solitary time that most people will ever experience in their lifetime, and yet, no one remembers it—no one that is, except parents, who bear silent witness to their newborn's solitary experience. This is no more true than with parents whom have had a child born significantly premature.

Children who are born prematurely are unique examples of the solitary early life. Full-term births are placed on a ward, perhaps with a panoramic observation window where parents and loved ones can look in and say how much like Mommy or Grandpa or Great-Uncle so and so they look. Not so with the *preemie*, whose first home is an *isolette* (formerly known as an incubator). The *isolette*, made of fiberglass, is a self-contained, temperature controlled, sterile, and stable breathing environment designed for life support and constant monitoring. Into this environment are significantly premature children born. They are, for the purposes of maintaining their fragile lives, *isolated* from contact with all but a highly specialized and uniquely trained neonatal intensive care unit (NICU) staff.

That first day of school will be a piece of cake, by comparison to this experience that they will not, but for the omnipresent living memory of their parents, ever remember themselves.

If these *preemies* could *consciously* draw on the experiences of their journey in the NICU, how much confidence in their ability to overcome obstacles could be gleaned? (I say *consciously* because no experience escapes the scrutiny of the subconscious). Think about the fact that these most fragile among us, in many cases, must struggle for the next breath, must endure and overcome taxing conditions to emerge alive and ready to move forward. What can life throw at them that will be more difficult than that?

Into this environment are preemies born and must endure until discharged. When they arrive, there are other mates in their room, some who have been there for a very long time. Those who have been there longest are lovingly referred to as the *grandfather/grandmother* of the unit. Theirs is the presence that greets new residents to the unit.

CHAPTER 1

THE INDEPENDENT

The commute home from midtown was, as usual, a hellish affair, with multiple train changes due to repairs to the Manhattan Bridge. It was my custom to take the uptown number "4" train to Times Square in order to get a seat on downtown "D" or the "Q" train, whichever came first. This would allow me the luxury of reading or snoozing, whatever the heat of the August day and my workload dictated. "Damn it," I say as I look down the tunnel and see the "Q" train, which is the express. The "Q" moves quickly and will get me closer to home, but it means a change for the local at the last express stop before mine. I get on and have my pick of seats, since the avalanche of human flesh that pours in when the doors open, doesn't happen until the next stop (42nd Street /5th Avenue). I grab a window seat, pull out a tech magazine, and plough into an article begun at lunchtime.

I look up when the doors open to the avalanche, smile a bit, and close my eyes and the magazine, enjoying the jostling and jockeying for the few remaining seats and door positions from the comfort of my perch by the window.

I close my eyes as the doors close on the Forty-Second Street station and settle in for a bit of a nap. I hear a young lady involved in, what is clearly a one-sided conversation, somewhere on my right. Looking up, I notice that she has a cell phone at her ear, and pray that someone will explain to her that there is no signal this far underground, but alas, no one does, and she drones on. She eventually stops, and silence is restored to the train car, and sweet sleep is again possible.

It seems that I can never sleep as the train crosses the bridge, and true to form, upon emerging from the Manhattan anchorage, my eyes pop open. The near twenty-minute nap always seems to invigorate, almost like taking a Wash-n-Dry to the back of my neck. I scrutinize the graffiti covered buildings of Chinatown and gaze down onto the impossibly backed up approaches to the Brooklyn Bridge and the roundabout to the Brooklyn Battery Tunnel. I never fail to ask myself how people could do this to themselves every day. Yes, there are a fair number of limos, and taxis, but there are also an inexplicably high number of people braving the traffic and daily driving into the city and all parts north.

That means paying for parking in Manhattan or forgoing the commuter rail lines and driving to and from Westchester and Connecticut. I've driven in from Brooklyn on very rare occasions, when there was no other reasonable alternative to the transportation conundrum, so I can speak to the madness involved in choosing to do it daily. I never fail to view that particular dynamic with disbelief and awe.

At the center of the span, the view never disappoints; the sun gleaming on the East River is truly a sight to behold. Sadness interrupts this delightful visage as I gaze down past the Brooklyn Bridge to the spot where the Twin Towers once stood, and ask myself the invariable and inevitable daily question, "How was this even possible?" We cross onto the Brooklyn anchorage and past the Jehovah's Witness' Watchtower complex, a well-maintained set of buildings in Northern Brooklyn, as we reenter the tunnel and darkness envelopes the train.

The conductor announces, "DeKalb Ave.," and a few people struggle toward the doors, which they must do because if they're too far from the doors when they open, the oncoming avalanche of human flesh will force them into an extra train stop. I smile and doze again knowing that from this point on the train will only become emptier because we've crossed the last big commuter center in the journey. My eyes open about ten minutes later after leaving the last express stop, and I'm in luck, we've just zoomed past a local, and I'll be able to catch it at the next express stop.

I get off at Church Ave. and cross the platform to await the arrival of the local, which I see in the near distance. The "D" train rumbles into the station minutes after the departure of the "Q," and I position myself to enter the second door of the eighth car.

The train rolls to a halt, and everything begins to move in slow motion when I behold a vision that completely takes my breath away. As I board the train, my head feels light, and I feel my heart beating harder, slower, and I am struggling to breathe. For the briefest moment, I think heart attack, but she sees me looking at her, smiled, and gave me a little Mr. Spok with her well-manicured eyebrows. At this point, I was able to begin my accustomed breathing activity once more. There was no smooth, convenient way to get near to her, even though the train was not crowded, and I did not wish to be obvious, so I lay back glancing occasionally, hoping to find opportunity to flash a friendly interested smile. In those moments, things began to move very quickly, and I did not know many things, but the one thing I did know was that I must have an opportunity to mash words with her. A plan began to formulate in my mind that would create the opportunity to exchange words with her. The next three subway stops on the IND line would run through what I considered my neighborhood.

Exiting at any one of the three would leave me with an easy walk home, so I resolved that if she exited at any one of them, I was prepared to do the same. Feeling only momentarily pleased with myself, having hatched a plan, my brain took the next logical step by asking, "And if she doesn't get off here, there, or there, then what?" Okay, the truth is, I was eminently prepared to travel to the end of the line at Brighton Beach should the situation require it. The conductor announced, "Beverly Rd.," as she sat quite comfortably. The distance between Beverly Rd. and the next stop, my stop, Cortelyou Rd. is quite short, so typically when the doors close at Beverly and the train begins to move, people seated gather their belongings and get up. To my everlasting delight, though she did not immediately get up, her body language suggested that the next stop, my stop, was also her stop.

These next few moments would require an enormous amount of delicate timing and precision. Too far behind would allow her off the train well before me with many others filling the space behind her; she'd be on her way up the stairs as I watched helplessly from below. I'd be asking myself upon exiting the station, "Where'd she go?" Too close would be obvious, and I don't like being obvious. Directly behind, out of eye line, that's where I need to be.

Did you ever see one of these jokers with the expensive designer leather briefcases? It serves many purposes in commuter culture. They use it to part the crowd, like Moses at the Red Sea, or to gesticulate or give directions, as if putting it on the ground and using their hands was somehow sacrilegious. Well, in New York, they're absolutely everywhere, waving that thing around, and making pedestrians lives miserable. They stick the thing out there, and who wants to collide with a briefcase, right? So most people just get out of the way and let the jerks go, not to get briefcase-bumped or create a confrontation.

The train stops at Cortelyou Rd., and the doors open; two people step off before her, and as she steps off, in the corner of my eye, I see a lovely brown Louis Vuitton valise rising to part the way. Instead of pulling this work of art back, it keeps coming, and at that moment, it occurs to me that he may have had a breathless, slow motion moment too, and I became determined that he should not be the beneficiary of the tonic which allowed me to resume my breathing activity. I stepped out, using the crush of humanity behind me, and drove his Louis Vuitton into the corner of the concrete stair. Well, he must've found his breath again because somewhere behind me I heard, "F——k"!

As we mount the stairs, I am able to assume a position right next to her and remark, "And it's not even hump day yet; this doesn't get any easier, does it?"

She smiles and says, "I guess you're right."

Returning her smile broadly, I say, "I'm Vonstone, and you are?"

"Loretta," she replied, "I'm Loretta."

We emerge into the August sunlight and the mild bustle of Cortelyou Rd. Pausing to gauge which direction she's leaning, my luck is holding because she's leaning left, and we stroll unhurriedly across Marlborough Rd. making meaningless neighborhood small talk as we go. We walk another block to Rugby Rd. at which point she announces, "This is my street," to which I reply, "I'm actually just there on the next street."

"Imagine that," she says, "you live on the very next street. Doubtless we will see one another again."

"It was indeed a pleasure meeting you, Loretta, and I do hope we see each other again very soon," I replied.

As we both shook hands and waved, I feigned to go into the bakery on the corner, but immediately stuck my head out to watch her walk down her street. Just then, I was chilled by a dreadful thought, Vonstone Wolfe, she's lived here for three years, and you have never seen her around the neighborhood. Damn it, you fool, you may never see her again. What you need is a plan to facilitate a high level mash of significant and meaningful words with her.

The next day I had, by all reports, a bounce in my step and nothing seemed to worry me. I cruised through the day with nary a care, and the only thing on my mind was the development of a scheme that would put me and Loretta face-to-face again. Typically, by 4:30 p.m., the only ones that remained in my department were me and my friend and coworker, Sammie. The two of us often talked about all kinds of stuff, especially affairs of the heart, so it was the most natural thing in the world for me to share the events of the previous evening with her.

I stroll around the wall to her desk. We often talked over the cubicle wall, but this was *Secret-Squirrel* stuff, so whispering was in order. I related to Sammie, in vivid and vibrant detail, the entire encounter and everything leading up to it. She stops what she's doing, and leaning forward on the desk, resting her head in her hands, seeming to hang on every word. She especially liked the briefcase chapter and couldn't stop laughing when the Louis Vuitton met the corner of the stair.

I complete the narrative and expressed my concerns about possibly never seeing her again.

"I know what I have to do, but if I do it, I'm a stalker," I tell her.

"You'll only be a stalker for a minute," she replied, "but if you do this right, you could have her forever. You *got to* do what you *got to* do, just don't get maced and wander dazed and confused into traffic, or you'll really never see her again, Vonstone."

I felt better about my plan and less and less a stalker.

"Thanks, Sammie, I'll keep you posted," I said.

"You'd better," Sammie replied. "I want details."

Tuesday, August 20, 2002, we both stepped off of the IND "Q" train together at 5:45 p.m., with "Louis Vuitton" cursing behind us. This should be a simple matter of timing, Vonstone. I simply have to present myself in the right place at the time that she emerges into the August sunset on Cortelyou Rd., and viola! The problem with theories is that you line up everything in exactly the same way in which you experienced success previously, but things don't often work out as predicted. Case in point, I left the office thirty minutes early for the remainder of the week in order to be in position to meet her train. Arriving in time to meet the two earlier trains, and remaining in place until four more trains had passed on each succeeding day, I realized by Tuesday that my plan was potentially flawed, so I went back to my sounding board, Sammie. I told Sammie that Loretta was somehow, through some diabolical methodology, circumventing *my* diabolical methodology.

"We can be devious even when we don't mean to be," said Sammie laughing.

Now with full disclosure here, if in your reading, this gives the appearance that I was stalking this nice young lady. Allow me to say in my defense that this was without a doubt the most flagrant act of stalking that I personally have ever witnessed. If I had become aware that someone else was doing this, the stick treatment may have become necessary. That being said, my goal was a five-minute conversation to determine if my rapidly beating heart and irregular breathing activity was symptomatic of something greater.

Having promulgated a perfectly logical scheme with nothing to show for it, I decided to shake things up a bit, so I skipped my Monday stalking vigil and went to the gym for a well-needed workout. Tuesday was cloudy and overcast with rain threatening, but I was determined to make a go of it, so I said goodbye to Sammie, bade her wish me luck and headed out early. Arriving home, I changed into casuals, took out my dinner, leaving it on the stove, and ventured back out into a light drizzle. I thought to myself, *I should go back for an umbrella; sage advice as it turned out*, but the urgency and excitement of the moment prevailed, and I jogged down toward the subway in an increasing, glasses-obscuring drizzle.

The five thirty-one was just pulling out of the station as the avalanche of flesh began pouring out onto Cortelyou Rd., umbrellas popping up as they emerge from the station. The rain had not yet begun in earnest, but my glasses were becoming a problem; if I had only listened to my little voice and turned back to get my umbrella. *Spilled milk*, I said wiping a droplet from the tip of my nose. I slipped into the grocery store next to the train station to buy a bottle of water and seek the shelter of their awning, but the mist simply drifted under the shelter and continued to soak me.

It suddenly occurred to me, as the five forty-one pulled into the station, that I had no good reason for standing here outside the train station in the rain. The jig would be up very quickly, despite my fervent desire not to appear obvious, if I couldn't concoct a plausible story explaining my presence here. Emerging from under the useless awning as the avalanche poured out of the station below, I see her ascending the stairs. She is wearing a sharp exquisitely tailored navy blue suit with a light blue broad-collared silk shirt opened to the second button. *Magnificent*, I thought to myself, *it seems that this creepy stalking behavior has paid off; breathe ... just breathe.*

As she walks past ducked under her umbrella. I say, "Loretta, hi, Vonstone, remember!"

She turns at the sound of her name with a puzzled and surprised look on her face, but she's smiling. Before she gathers a response, I say emphatically, "It seems that we are destined to meet each other around trains."

Through the puzzled smile, she manages, "What are you doing out here in the rain?" turning up her one available palm and glancing toward the sky.

"I'm waiting for my mom. But I suspect that, because of the developing weather, she's skipped the train and had my dad pick her up instead," I said with my most sincere voice.

"Hmm," she said nodding her head once to the side.

I can't tell whether that meant that she was impressed, and that she bought my story, or she was quietly trying to remember if she switched her can of mace into this pocketbook. I fall in beside her as she offers me shelter under the umbrella and her shoulder tucks inside mine. We begin to walk unhurriedly up Cortelyou Rd., away from the Independent, which was still spilling human cargo into the street on its journey to the sea.

Typically. Sammie and I would talk when everyone had gone for the day, but there was too much ground to cover, so as soon as I got in, I said, "You eat, Sammie?"

Sammie said she hadn't, so we hit the elevator and headed down to La Cuccina, an overpriced bistro on the lower level of the MetLife Building. "So ... tell me! Don't make me beat it out of you!" said Sammie unusually impatiently, "and don't leave anything out."

I related the events of the prior evening to her in vivid and illustrative fashion, omitting no detail no matter how small, beginning with my early departure from work the prior day. After twenty minutes or so, we realized that this was a longer conversation than we had allotted time for, so we rose simultaneously and began to make our way back with me still spilling details.

Lunch was typically a communal affair with fifteen or so people from three departments gathering in the big conference room, so we were left with after work again. Several of the younger guys would get together after hours and play some server based killing game, but being engrossed in the murder and mayhem of the game, they basically ignored us. Picking up where I left off, I related the rest of the evening adventure with all of the excruciating detail that my audience demanded. When the tale was completed, the only thing that Sammie said was, "Well, no mace, burning eyes, and wandering dazed into traffic? Success, by any measure!"

To which I replied, "It was really touch and go there for a couple of seconds though."

CHAPTER 2

INTO THE BREACH: THE FUNNEL

The long awaited, much anticipated, and highly orchestrated mash of words went off without a hitch, and produced the most favorable results imaginable. She took my phone number and promised to call. We spoke on a range of issues that were important to both of us. About a week later, as I was replying to some emails at home, my phone rings.

"Hello," I answered.

"Hello, Vonstone, it's Loretta."

"Well, hello," I said, wondering if I sounded overly delighted.

We chatted for more than an hour, during which she gave me her number. Somewhere in the middle of our long chat, Loretta told me that she was hosting an affair at her apartment that Saturday, and I promised to provide the flowers for the event. I don't mean to suggest that I was in any way *invited* to the soiree, you understand, but I wanted to do whatever I could to be *helpful*.

I had some errands that took me into Manhattan on Saturday morning and met a friend in Park Slope for lunch as I worked my way back home. After lunch, I visited one of the myriad of flower shops on Seventh Ave. and purchased all the white carnations that they had. On my way home, I rang up Loretta, no answer. I had a soiree of my own to attend at the home of a work colleague, so upon arriving at home, I quickly showered, dressed, and headed back out to get wine. As I drove down Cortelyou Rd., I saw Loretta in a hair salon chatting with someone, which I thought a bit ironic, owing to the fact that Loretta has no hair.

I hurriedly parked and retrieved the flowers from the trunk. As I approached, smiling with this huge cache of white carnations, her friend saw me and touched her arm, calling her attention to my approach. As she turned, she smiled and said, "Oh, thank you so very much. You really saved me a trip."

"It was my pleasure. Can I do anything else to help?" I say beaming.

"No, I've got everything covered, and just need to go home and get ready," says the lady with the perfectly manicured nails.

"Well, you know I could ..."

"I'm sure you could," she said cutting me off, smiling. "Have a good time, and I want to see pictures," I said.

"Thanks," she said smiling broadly.

Returning to my car, I checked the rear view as I drove off, and yup, she looked.

Because we were both in a place where we'd each been down the serious-relationship road a few times, we wanted to establish the ground rules before going on to another. The central issue for us both was the fact that we both *absolutely* wanted to have children; and likewise, we both currently had none. I was a gentleman of a certain age, and she a lady of somewhat less than a certain age. We were both from the Caribbean and proudly so, but appreciating that we lived in the cultural hub of the western hemisphere. Coolest of all, we lived around the corner from one another, which would really come in handy later.

The science of pharmacology is a wonderful discipline, especially when they can be applied to solving human problems, and not just treating symptoms. Despite being two healthy adults with eminently compatible and fully functioning equipment, we were unable to conceive (certainly not for a lack of exuberant effort). So after exploring and exhausting the full range of natural approaches, and a fair amount of what can only be reasonably described as sheer quackery, we took the next logical step, we went to see a fertility *specialist.* We went to several fertility *specialists;* everyone had a *specialist* that they swore was *"the"* guy. Nutshell: we did two rounds of *artificial insemination* with an ungodly nightly cocktail of drugs (which produced a dizzying array of physical symptoms), purchased at even unholier expense, all without result; well, no good results anyway. After the second round of punishing nightly injections failed to produce a result, Loretta and I made the decision to try something else. A friend suggested an IVF clinic on Central Park South where some good results were being had by eager couples, so we made an appointment.

The neighborhood that we lived in was a quaint mixture of stately Victorian homes with a smattering of apartment buildings built between the 1940s and the 1960s. The ribbon that held it all together was Cortelyou Rd., which ran right down the middle. There was quite a pulse on that strip, and it was getting stronger all the time as the older residents died off, moved away, or just ventured out less and less. There were a couple of very good restaurants that opened in the neighborhood with the promise of many more to come as well as a Saturday farmer's market. All in all, this went from a good place to live to an exciting place to live in pretty short order. There was one restaurant in particular that was, for a brief moment in time, the hub of activity in our community.

Loretta and I frequented this restaurant weekly as we were quite fond of several items on the menu. Loretta was uniquely fond of one specific dish, the bread pudding. I must admit that this was, without a doubt, the best bread pudding that I have ever experienced. We would always culminate a meal by sharing a generous slice drizzled with guava rum sauce, followed by a walk around the neighborhood's quiet streets.

There is an inexplicable pall of quiet desperation that lingers in the waiting room of a fertility clinic; it is palpable and slips onto you like a cold, damp overcoat when you enter the waiting room. Many fertility practices decorate in such a way as to attempt to cheer, distract, and/or otherwise lift the pall, but despite their best efforts in decor, they are the most universally cheerless and dire places on earth. This well-addressed clinic was no different in that respect.

There were seven or eight couples in the waiting room, all observing a queer ritual of facing one another and avoiding eye contact with anyone else. It's almost as if they were feeding on each other's hope, hope that could be found nowhere else but in each other's eyes.

The consultation with the doctor is routine, but he makes us feel as if this isn't the twelve-thousandth time he has done this, and this somehow helps to take the edge off of the experience. He explains the process to us in painful detail, outlining for the two neophytes who just told him that we did two rounds of AI—the role that we must each play. We are made to understand the egg retrieval process as well as the sperm *"production"* procedure. They show me to *the room*, where I do my part, and we make an appointment for an early morning egg retrieval.

As with our prior artificial insemination efforts, as well as our own *natural* endeavors, which we pursued with *perpendicular cataclysm*, we were always singularly hopeful about the result. We felt as if each endeavor would be the one to produce our desired result. Even when we didn't achieve a good outcome, we always felt that "if not this, then next thing, or the one after that." We approached IVF with the same energy and enthusiasm. When the first round of IVF proved absolutely fruitless, I stepped back to take a look at where we were.

The most devastating three words that a couple, seeking help through science to conceive, can hear are *"it didn't take."* Those simple three words, put together in that combination and whispered into a telephone receiver, have the power to shatter, to ruin a day, or to send an aspiring young mother crying into the nearest restroom.

I mentally assessed the drug toll that the process was taking on Loretta, and for the first time. I had a question in my mind; the hitherto unspoken question, "should we go on?"

The question was a weight that fell to the floor between us (I swear it made a sound). Okay, it's out in the open where it can be seen, heard, evaluated, and summarily dismissed, first by Loretta, then shaken off by me a moment later. She had to be first in this; after all, the physical toll, the incredible physical burden was hers and hers alone to bear. Though I wish that I could help carry it, but

I could only offer comfort, and big t-shirts. I could only share the emotional burden, but the physical tally fell uniquely to my lady. I was able to secure from her one concession—we agreed to take a break. Enjoy some things that didn't involve injections, egg retrievals, and stroking off.

Loretta is from a large family, having two surviving sisters and two brothers. She and her sister, Lorraine, are particularly close. Lorraine, who lives in Guyana (South America), was blessed with three children, all of whom have a close relationship with their aunt Loretta. They all touch base regularly, so Lorraine was keenly aware of the struggle we were having conceiving, I could tell, from the part of the conversation to which I was privy, that our situation quite pained Lorraine, as they were both often in tears. One Sunday afternoon, as I was preparing dinner, the telephone rang, it was Lorraine.

"Hey, sis, how are you," I said?

"Fine, fine, Von, just coming from church. I want you to know that I continue to pray for you and Loretta," she said.

"Thanks, sis, that means a lot," I responded, "I'll get Loretta."

The conversation unfolded in the den, so I had no access, but when Loretta came into the kitchen to hang up the phone, she was smiling as she looked at me.

"What?" I said half smiling.

"My sister has offered to carry for us."

"What'd you tell her?" I asked expectantly.

"I thanked her and told her I love her for offering, but I can do it. We can do it."

I reached out and hugged her close, and told her how much I loved her. Dinner was a little burned that Sunday afternoon as we were moved to distraction with great vigor.

We enjoyed meeting in the city after work and eating at some of our favorite restaurants, and shopping. We particularly enjoyed Friday night takeout and a movie; in general, all the things that make living in New York special. We resumed all aspects of our pre-fertility experience, including regular vigorous, unpressured, and gratuitous sex, usually after the aforementioned takeout and copious amounts of wine. On the weekend, we'd breakfast at one of the increasing number of neighborhood restaurants, or I'd make us a big breakfast at home, after which we might venture out to the farmers market. The time we spent was so special and carefree, but behind it all was the burning, burgeoning question, yeah, you know the one.

In the wee small hours of a Saturday morning in mid-July 2004, I got up to go to the bathroom. When I got back into the bed, I noticed that Loretta was awake. She propped up on her elbow, which usually meant that she wanted to talk. At this point, we were about three months into our hiatus, and I was on the point of initiating a discussion of resuming our fertility efforts.

"It's been almost three months," she said.

"I know, I was just thinking the same thing before I fell asleep last night," I said. "We should give the clinic a call on Monday," I said before she could reply.

I see her teeth gleaming in the darkness and sensed that I was the odd man out on some important piece of information.

"We may want to hold off on that," she said almost cryptically. "It seems that my period is late, and you know how ..."

"Yes I know, clockwork; how late?" I said.

"Four days," she replied. "I didn't want to sound the alarm because with all the drugs, I wanted to allow for the possibility that they may have thrown me off," said Loretta.

We've been down this road a couple of times, only to have our hopes dashed by a red spot in the middle of the night, so I understand Loretta's hesitancy to call it. We stop at the drug store later in the day to pick up a home pregnancy test kit, and for the first time, we say the words, almost together, "We're pregnant."

On Monday, Loretta phoned into the OB/GYN for an appointment, and they slotted us in for Tuesday afternoon at 2:00 p.m. We walked to the office, as was our custom, owing to the fact that it was only three blocks away, and upon arriving, we signed in and were led immediately to the ultrasound room. It seemed as if we'd done this a thousand times before, though it was never quite routine. We always held hands with a feeling of great anticipation and expectation. So, afterward, as we sat in the doctor's office for the post ultrasound consult, we're greeted the words "Congratulations, you're pregnant."

With a knowing glance, we squeeze each other's hand, and smile. I remember musing to myself, *How many times he's said this today?* Not that it mattered one little bit because this was the first time that *we'd* heard it together.

There was a guarded sense of relief and accomplishment felt between us at having finally achieved pregnancy without having to return to the dreaded fertility regimen of injected drugs. The walk home was completed in almost total silence; lots of hugging and *cat that stole the canary* type smiling at each other. We'd been living with great likelihood of pregnancy for a few days (since the pregnancy test) and thought that we'd grown accustomed to the *idea*, but there's something about a trusted medical professional's imprimatur to *make it, at long last, real.* *"Congratulations, you're pregnant"*—sweetest words ever.

We began to behave as I imagine pregnant couples behave, though we'd been through the process many times, without good result, there seemed to be an unspoken and electric optimism alive in this pregnancy, as well as in us; and it put a proverbial bounce in our every step. We unconsciously began to speak expectantly and inclusively when we talked of the future. I purchased two books that dealt specifically with nursery décor because I had some great ideas on what I wanted this room to look like (provided that our child is a boy). That future now included a non-descript and growing mass of hope shielded and protected inside Loretta's body.

Based on Loretta's history, Dr. Kelly felt the need to have a robust monitoring routine. If any trends should develop, we wanted to be aware of them early in order to access whatever preventive or stabilizing measures were available at that stage. Therefore, we began the routine of weekly ultrasounds, which we minded not in the least because each contact brought us closer to this tiny life being nurtured inside Loretta. So we made the weekly three block trek to the OB/GYN to see our baby. We made the conscious decision not to share our great news with anyone outside our tight family circle. The decision was a good one, but it was killing me to keep the biggest secret of my life.

Sitting at my desk one afternoon, Sammie strolls by on her way back from the restroom and asks quite matter-of-factly, "How's Loretta?"

This caught me a bit off guard as I thought we'd pick up where we left off chatting about the latest round of severance packages that were being offered by our company. Everyone secretly hoped to be offered a package, but though I was eminently eligible, I wasn't disposed either way. To Sammie's question, I very nearly reply, "She's pregnant."

Sammie, being the first person with whom I shared the details of how Loretta and I met on the Independent as well as the intricacies of the stalk/woo/win plan, obviously held a special place of confidence with me. It felt a bit weird, maybe even a bit dishonest keeping this from her. "Once again, Vonstone, how—is—Loretta?" she said.

Being careful now and in full and undistracted command of my senses and speech, I said, "Fine mostly, but mornings have been a little rough lately."

I know, I should have just gone with she's pregnant. After she hugs and congratulates me, I swear her to secrecy just as another coworker strolls up and asks, "Don't tell anybody what, and am I anybody?"

"*Shit.*"

This was not going to be easy, especially working with a bunch of women who are tuned in on every frequency.

Typically, Loretta would attend church on Sunday, but since mornings were problematic, Sundays being no exception, Sunday mornings were largely spent in bed or on the comfy leather sofa in the den. I'd stay close to home, working in the house or around the yard on one project or the other and start dinner around one o'clock or thereabouts. As I was setting up the cooking playlist, the telephone rang. Catching it on the third ring, "Hello."

It was Loretta's pastor giving a powerful example of "the mountain coming to Mohammed" corollary. I took the phone to Loretta in the den, and they spoke for about five minutes. When she came into the kitchen, she reported to me that we were to expect a visit from twelve church members. This I already knew, but the flipside of that record is that when church folks come visiting after church on Sunday, you've got to feed them.

"This is one case where your cooking for an army may just pay off," said Loretta.

"It'll be close, but I think we'll be okay," I said.

When I cook a meal, any meal, I usually cook enough so that we can have leftovers for two days, and one lunch, so there's always enough food. This is always the case, especially when I cook one of our favorite meals. This particular Sunday, I was preparing Loretta's favorite meal, oxtail with rice and peas, so there was plenty of food. Our impromptu guests arrived at about three o'clock, and while they chatted with Loretta in the living room, I laid the buffet in the dining room. Opening the sliding doors leading from living room to the dining room, I announced, "Dinner is served."

I directed everyone toward the restroom to freshen up while I retrieve the cloth napkins from the sideboard, and fold them quickly.

The pastor blessed the meal and Loretta and I, and our guests ate their fill, some even having seconds. One even remarking how much she liked the oxtail and that it tasted "just like hers." The eyes of her husband, who sat right behind her, popped open, and he slowly and discretely shook his head causing me to smile and leaving her with the impression that I felt complimented by her words. Having been very well fed, our little troupe retreated down the stairs and out into the beautiful August afternoon. Loretta never again complained about me cooking too much food.

Monday morning came, as Monday mornings do, as a total surprise. Though I go to bed on Sunday evening with the knowledge that I have to get up and go to work the next day, Monday morning never fails to take me by surprise. I don't view Monday in any kind of a bad light you understand, because I feel that Mondays generally get a bad rap, but Mondays always catch me unexpected. I roll out of bed, leaving Loretta tightly bundled under the covers, and head for the bathroom to run the shower and get it steamy. Showering and shaving quickly, I always leave myself a few minutes to enjoy the hot bathroom as the A/C cycles to 75°F for the morning.

Dressing quickly, I stand in the bedroom door looking in at Loretta.

"We can't," she says, "besides you're already dressed."

"Now you know ..." I say before she cuts me off.

"You're going to be late."

Tomorrow, I wake up fifteen minutes earlier, I tell myself. That's our time. I head for the kitchen where the coffee is brewing. I strap on an apron and whip up a six-egg omelet, half of which I leave for Loretta when she gets up. I eat it standing in the den looking out onto Cortelyou Rd., which is alive with commuters heading for the trains in one direction and the commuter busses to Manhattan in the other. I reminisce about the mornings that I stood in this very spot hoping to catch a glimpse of Loretta as she walked purposefully up Cortelyou Rd. to catch the commuter bus. I finish off the omelet and the last of the coffee and head for the bathroom. I stop in the room and rub her bottom under the covers.

"Are you sure you don't want some of this, mister?"

"You're terrible, I should jump in there just for spite," I chide. "Call you later," I say kissing her head.

She mumbles something purposefully unintelligible, and I am out of the house and on the street.

The office seems unusually empty this morning, and I have to remind myself that this is what happens in a merger. Addressing duplication in services is usually the first order of business. As I sit down and drop my bag on the desk, my phone rings, "This is Vonstone," I answer.

I look at the caller ID, and it's my friend in HR. He says, "Good, you're there, meet me across the street in five," and hangs up.

I know exactly what this means. He's giving me a heads up that I'm to be made an offer for a package. We meet in the breezeway to Park Av., and he hands me a bag with a muffin.

"Thanks, but I could've come to your office to get this," I say.

"That one knock 'em down over at the comedy club last night?" I smile and gaze down the breezeway onto Park Av. at all the limos in front of the Waldorf Astoria.

"The list with the latest round is hot off the Xerox, and you feature prominently my friend," he said.

"Any idea of a timeline?" I ask.

"Best guess, I'd say the end of next week at the latest," he replies.

"Hey, you figure to have a pretty busy and expensive morning, running up and down delivering all this grim reaper news," I joke.

"Eleven years, man; you and me," he says.

"Let's go, James Bond, before someone sees us, and thanks for the heads up. You're a friend," I tell him.

"No thanks necessary. How's the missus?"

"She's great. I'm going to check on her when I go back up," I reply.

We walk back into the building separately through separate security checkpoints. This is really necessary because he could be fired for what he just did. I call Loretta as soon as I sit down and deliver the news in code. We talk no more about it just then, but chat about other things until the doorbell rings. She takes the phone to the door with her and announces that our neighbor, Jeanne, has popped over. I ask her to tell Jeanne hi for me and ring off. Jeanne is the best; she's always dropping over with baked goodies to satisfy Loretta's sweet tooth. I sign on and promulgate my already prepped departure plan, with several well-constructed macros, that transfer everything I needed to a memory stick, emailed everything previously flagged to my personal email address, while deleting everything of a personal nature. I'm ready.

The week goes by pretty uneventfully, until I get a call on Friday from my VP. He hasn't called me since the days I reported directly to him, so when I hear his voice, I know that the wheels are in motion. I'm glad that he's the one that brings the message because I have a unique opportunity to set the parameters for my departure. We chat in his office for about thirty minutes, and the unexpected happens. He offers me a position in an umbrella company, but his offer is an absolute non-starter because I had no respect for the fellow to whom I'd be reporting. The severance package was a much better option.

I meet with the HR representative for IT and receive the details of my package. I know that Monday or Tuesday at the very latest would mark the end of days for me at the company. I spend the remaining time, as per my request, handing over projects with detail statuses and deliverables for reassignment and cruising around saying goodbye to colleagues. No one can believe that I know the day and nearly the hour of my departure. In my conversation with the VP, I said that I came in on my own, and I'd like to continue to work until I have done my handover; so when the moment came, I didn't suffer the indignity of having a security guard hovering over me at my desk. My manager chirped my phone, as prearranged, and I went to his office, shook his hand, handed in my credentials and technology, and left on my own. As one who has seen many departures, it felt good. I went to MJ's for a scotch and ginger, and headed for the Independent.

The IND was empty, lonely, and devoid of soul. I wasn't used to experiencing it in this way. It afforded me time to think, to reflect on the past week, month, twelve years that I had spent working there, and just then I realized that just like when some*one* dies, or a relationship dies, one likewise needs to mourn, of sorts, when a situation comes to an end. I hadn't allowed myself to think about it quite in that way, and I wished I had. But this time was as good as any to begin the process; to begin to heal.

It's one of those strange days where the sun is shining in some places, but not in others. I emerge from the train station, and it is cloudy where I am, but two blocks away, the sun has illuminated PS 139. I catch myself walking quickly, then remind myself that, though it's the middle of a workday, I am not working now, so slow down. I'm not really hungry, but I know that Loretta would appreciate some shrimp Parmesan from San Remo, so I stop and place an order. I also stop and pick up a slice of bread pudding. Loretta is waiting when I arrive and she says, "You okay?"

"You know, I thought I was, but I realize that I didn't put enough thought into it, so I've got to give myself some time to process this," I say. "Listen, I brought lunch."

"Sushi?"

"No, Italian."

"Shrimp parmesan?" she asks.

I nod and say, "Our baby is going to look like shrimp Parmesan." We both crack up.

The holidays were always a special and highly anticipated time with me; a time for family, food, and fellowship. The 2004 edition, however, was shaping up to be somewhat different since Loretta had recently been placed on bed rest by Dr. Kelly. In 2003, we hosted my entire family at our house for Christmas dinner. It was magnificent in all of its chaos, and when it was over, we said to each other, "We're never doing *that* again." So when the holidays rolled around, all things considered, we knew that it'd be fairly low key. Thanksgiving was a breeze of simplicity, by our standards anyway, two meats four sides, one desert and coffee. This was the easiest Thanksgiving ever, quiet and intimate with just John and Rosetta. Christmas was the same, but Loretta and I visited some friends who typically have a raucous mostly girl affair on Christmas night. It was more raucous than I'd remembered from the prior year, and after packing in all the fun and sidesplitting laughter that we could in the pre-allotted two-hour window, we headed for home.

We were supposed to spend New Year's Eve in New Jersey with my cousin and his family and an intimate gathering, consuming conspicuous amounts of sushi.

The *secret* of the pregnancy having been revealed to a few well-chosen family members, who then propagated it like something akin to wildfire; they promised Loretta a special place buttressed by many comfortable pillows to lounge for the evening. Early New Year's Eve, however, Loretta began to feel a bit strange. She was not able to describe or localize the sensation with any accuracy, but felt that she'd be better off in bed. "I'm that glad you agree," she said, "but you should go and have a good time for both of us."

You know what that was, don't you? That is without a doubt the oldest trap in the book of traps that womenfolk spring on unsuspecting menfolk. The wrong response could see me into the doghouse for some time to come, and then on a short leach, thereafter, for some unspecified period of time. "Honey, don't be silly, there is no other place more important for me to be than right here, with you, right now, and that is that. I'm calling Gordon to let him know what the situation is, okay?" I said.

"Okay," she said with a comforted smile.

With that, I picked up the phone and informed my cousin that we wouldn't be making it and wished everyone a happy New Year. I put two bottles of sparkling cider into the fridge to chill, put some Costco horse's ovaries in the oven, and climbed into bed and cuddled. Living in New York was great for a whole host of reasons, the absolute least of which was going to Times Square on New Year's Eve. I'd lived there for forty years, and had been to Times Square hundreds of times, from the Looking at the undulating throng in Times Square, I recall the days when the landscape was dominated by various aspects of the porn industry, until the latter day where everything was a gleaming tourist trap of fake blues clubs, faux theatres, and casual fast food joints of every description. However, in all that time, I had never been there on New Year's Eve; and the truth be known in all of its glory, I don't know *anyone* who had. I never failed to look out on that throng, from the safety and comfort of my living room, or my bed, and wonder out loud, *Who are those people?*

So, being typical New Yorkers, we watched the spectacle unfold on TV with Dick Clark, or a reasonable facsimile thereof, and consumed the bubbly apple juice. The traditional midnight calls were made and received, and we settled in for a winter's night sleep. Loretta spent New Year's Day resting in bed while I puttered about the house. The pressure she was feeling the night before continued unabated, and we agreed that I'd call the midwife-on-call as soon as we finished lunch. I soon placed the call, and within thirty minutes, the midwife, a Reubenesque Norwegian woman named Inga, called back. Once I told her what was going on, she told us to come in at 8:00 a.m. on Monday, but in the meantime, I was to keep her comfortable and report of any changes.

On Monday morning, bright and early, we presented ourselves at Dr. Kelly's office and were ushered to the ultrasound room by Inga.

"So how you feeling this morning; you taking it easy?" asked Inga.

"I feel as if large hands are gently applying pressure to my lower abdomen," replied Loretta.

31

"S'gonna be cold, okay?" said Inga as she squeezed the cold KY-Jelly onto Loretta's belly.

Because we were the first appointment of the day, the jelly had not had a chance to warm up. Inga moves the probe about in the slippery stuff, and I see her brow knit with concern. Before I could ask, she prints the picture, rips it off, and says, "Be right back, okay?" As she dashes from the room, Loretta and I look silently at each other. Moments later, Dr. Kelly enters the room and after viewing the screen, he asks Loretta to get dressed and join him in his office.

Before we could sit, Dr. Kelly said, "I'd like you to see someone. Her name is Dr. Sandra Velella, and she's a top perinatalogist."

"Why, what's wrong?"

"I am seeing what I believe to be an advance of the funneling that caused me to recommend bed rest," said Dr. Kelly.

"How advanced, and at what point in the pregnancy would you expect to see *funneling?*" I asked.

"I'd expect to see this progression within a few weeks or so of delivery. Here's the address, Dr. Velella is holding nine o'clock for you, so you'd better get going," he said.

We look at each other, stand up together, thank Dr. Kelly, and we leave the office.

CHAPTER 3

IT'S GRAVITY BABY

Sandra Velella was a short, dark haired urgent woman with piercing, probing, yet understanding eyes. Her movements were quick and deliberate, raising the level of confidence around her in-patient and staff alike. As promised, the clinic was holding nine o'clock for us. As we walked in and made eye contact with the front desk clerk, she said, "Are you Loretta, Loretta Lawrence?"

"Yes we are," I said, feeling a bit clumsy with my response. "Please take a seat and someone will be out to get you shortly, but in the meantime, sir, would you start ..."

"Be happy to," I said cutting her off and rising from my seat to retrieve the clipboard that she was *about* to offer.

Loretta shot me a look; she hates when I force people off script, but I glory in it. I'm about half way through the forms when the technician calls out, "Loretta Lawrence?"

I clam up this time and let the lady answer to her own name.

I complete the forms in the examining room while the technician sets up the sonogram machine. She explains to us that this sonogram is a bit different in that it is 3D. "This should be different," I say looking over at Loretta, who is completely oblivious to me, the technician, and her surroundings. She has quietly slipped inside, and is exploring her own thoughts; I shut up. The technician performs the scan, and when it's complete she says, "There *he* is ..." then she suddenly looks nervously over at us. I sense her concern and reply smiling, "It's okay, we already knew the sex."

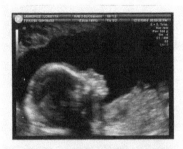

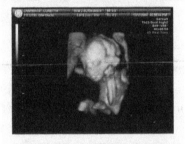

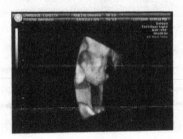

3D Image of Joshua

She looks relieved as she grabs the picture of our son and zooms out of the room, leaving us staring at this magnificent 3D image on the screen. We gaze at it in silence as I am completely lost for words, and Loretta is … well … inside.

After five minutes or so, Dr. Velella comes in and introduces herself. She reiterates Dr. Kelly's concern and explains that the situation is quite alarming. We're floored when she says that Loretta will need to be hospitalized immediately. *Wow*, we certainly did not expect that, but Loretta takes it quite in stride.

"Can you make this happen," Dr. Velella asks?

"I just need to make a few phone calls to get it set up," Loretta replies.

"I'll get you a room on the maternity ward. It should hopefully only take about an hour or so," says Dr. Velella.

We leave the clinic and head home to make calls and arrangements. Loretta calls her manager, who is was already on notice, and he immediately made the appropriate notification to HR and just like that, the wheels were set in motion. By one-thirty, we're checking into the hospital. My head is spinning, but Loretta is a sea of tranquility in all of the chaos. She appeared to be in a zone.

A PCT (personal care tech) dropped by with Loretta's new patient care package. She was quite pleasant and engaging and introduced herself warmly.

"Hi, I'm Gloria, and I'm going to take care of you. Whenever I can help, just press the call button, and I'll get you whatever you need."

"Thank you so much, Gloria," I said. "I know that this was kind of a short notice admission, but has the doctor sent over any notes, or a treatment plan of any kind?"

"Your nurse will be in to talk to you about all of that in a few minutes. Remember, if you need anything, let me know," said Gloria her voice trailing as she left the room.

"Well," I said, "I guess this is it," as I drew the curtain and Loretta began to undress.

As she lay back in the bed, I grabbed an extra pillow and placed it behind her and started to adjust the bed up when the charge nurse entered the room with a knock.

"You goin' the wrong way, baby," she said as she drew back the curtain. "My name is Linda, and I'm your nurse until 11:00," she said introducing herself. "I've got to read you the riot act. I'm going to give you all the dos and don'ts, mostly don'ts sad to say. The first big *don't* is don't be vertical, and the second is, don't be horizontal," said Linda almost cryptically.

We both looked at each other rather quizzically, but inherently understood that this woman must know what she's talking about, so I chuckled politely and bade her *"splain."* Looking straight at Loretta, she explained.

"Gravity is not your friend. It pulls everything toward the earth. Right now, it's pulling your baby to earth, so we're going to fight it by flipping you."

"For a few hours a day, or while she sleeps?" I ask.

Still looking at Loretta, she says, "Twenty-four-seven, for as long as you're here."

With that, Linda moved over and readjusted the bed into a seemingly impossible sleep position. "This is how you'll look at the world until you deliver," as she pressed the buttons on the bed, it leveled off and began to tilt back until Loretta's head was lower than her feet by twenty-seven degrees. "I'm not *showing* you how to do this, understand, but it might be convenient to know."

"I u-n-d-e-r-s-t-a-n-d," I said nodding my head.

Nurse Linda went over some other don't(s), such as don't get up without assistance, don't try to lay horizontal, don't attempt to sit in a chair, don't walk around, and the biggest *don't* of all, don't sit on the toilet. "Until you deliver that baby, *gravity is your enemy*, so we will fight it with every tool at our disposal, so," she said, now looking at me, "help us to help give your baby a fighting chance; are you with me?"

"I'm all in," I said looking at Loretta. "This position is called Trendelenburg position; it is designed to use gravity to keep the little fella inside, so whatever you two have to do ..."

The hospital is a great place to deal with what's ailing you, but it can be a cold, lonely, and uncertain place; I saw this within minutes of admission. As a consequence, I made a decision that I was going to leave Loretta alone as little as humanly possible. I was going to make her send me home, and then I'd always come back. She had to stay there; she was stuck, so I wanted to offer her a fixed point on which she could depend. As I began to fold her street clothes and put them into a bag, Gloria the PCT came in to ask if Loretta was hungry, to which Loretta replied that she'd wait for dinner.

"Well, if you get hungry, either of you, we almost always have sandwiches, salads, juice, coffee, or tea in the hospitality room fridge next door," she says.

I left after dinner and headed for the gym for a quick work-out, after which I stopped by the folks to give them an update. Of course, my mom wanted to know when she could visit. I told her that Loretta needed to settle in, and I'd let her know as soon as it was possible. After taking care of a few things at home, including some forgotten items (cell phone charger and reading materials), I headed back to the hospital for a night visit. Parking would always be a problem at Maimonides Hospital, but I realized quickly that because I was not limited in the hours that I could visit, I either arrive just after 10:00 p.m., when visiting hours ended, or at about 11:30 p.m. after the hospital shift change.

"What are you doing back here?" she said as I walked in bearing gifts. "Did you bring my charger?"

"Yes, I did," I said proudly. "How was dinner?" I asked.

"Awful," she said making a face.

"How's the Trendelenburg thing going?" I ask.

She gives me the look.

"The nurse says that you'll see Dr. Velella in the morning," I tell her. "She will be able to give us some more details about your stay as well as what they expect. I'm going to be here a lot, so if you thought that this was some kind of vacation from me, you've got another thing coming ma'am," I say with a smile. I sit with her until she dozes off talking and then I head home.

The house feels empty, lonely, and almost echo(y). After a nice long hot shower, which always makes me feel better, I spend about an hour making calls and bringing people up to speed before dozing off talking to someone. I awake at six o'clock because, in addition to the parking situation, I am determined not to miss Dr. Velella when she makes her appearance. Her clinic is right down the street, and I surmise that she will stop by before her appointments commence at 8:00 a.m. I make a thermos of hazelnut decaf and head out "back roading" it all the way.

The parking gods are with me, and there is abundant parking at the rear of the hospital. It's quite cold as I turn up my collar and push both hands deep into the pockets of my coat, holding the thermos under my arm. Arriving on the second floor, I bid good morning to the nurses at the station, who ignore me as they are in the midst of their shift change. Loretta is awake and gazing out the window as the PCT takes her temperature and blood pressure. "Morning, sunshine, did you rest well?" I ask.

The PCT wraps up and leaves as Loretta responds saying, "Morning, early bird, find any worms on your way in? I slept surprisingly well last night; must have been tired."

"You surely were," I said. "You dozed off mid-sentence."

"Yours or mine?" she said.

"Mine, I think, but I got even; I think I dozed off on one of your friends," I replied.

"You didn't."

"Oh I can assure you I did," I said.

"Who was it. do you remember who?" asked Loretta?

"I don't know," I said.

"I'm hoping we'll be able to speak with Dr. Velella this morning. As I spoke the words, who should walk in but Dr. Kelly?"

"Good morning folks. Loretta, how are you doing?" said Dr. Kelly.

"I'm quite well, Dr. Kelly. We are hoping to see Dr. Velella this morning to get a sense of the game plan," said Loretta.

"I spoke with her yesterday at length regarding your situation, and she's going to stop by this morning. She should actually be here now, based on our conversation."

Dr. Kelly came all the way in, and I relinquished my seat at Loretta's bedside to make room for the doctor. As they talked about the virtues of Trendelenburg, I stepped into the hall for a bit. I was there for only a couple of minutes when I heard an urgent footfall making its way down the hall. Before turning to the direction of the sound, I knew that it had to be the expected Dr. Sandra Velella.

The doctors presented on either side of the Trendelenburg(ed) patient where Loretta conceded that the position was somewhat uncomfortable but bearable.

Dr. Velella said, "Loretta, Trendelenburg is only the beginning. It will be necessary to take further steps to stretch out this pregnancy for as long as humanly possible."

"I understand," said Loretta.

"What are some of these steps you mentioned Dr. Velella?" I inquired.

"The first thing that we'll do is to perform a procedure called a *cervical cerclage*. Because of your prior reproductive history, and your *incompetent cervix*, Loretta, we'll need to help it retain your baby. The cerclage involves placing stitches in the cervix to keep it closed for as long as possible. This works in conjunction with Trendelenburg and medications like magnesium sulfate, and other tocolytics, to treat preeclampsia," said Dr. Velella.

"Are there generally good outcomes when all the steps you just outlined are put into place?" I ask.

"Let me be honest with you, Mr. Wolfe, in Loretta's situation, our goal is to buy time, hopefully its months, failing that weeks, or even days. You guys are smart enough to know that there are no guarantees with this kind of business, but we'll do all that we can to fight for every minute inside that we can, fair enough?" said Dr. Velella.

"Fair enough," we said in chorus.

Dr. Kelly, whose contribution to this point had been a succession of agreeing nods, rose and indicated that he had to leave, but said that he'd be dropping by mornings, and would always be available on his cell.

"I've got to go as well, Loretta, but I'll schedule the cerclage for Thursday, okay?" said Dr. Velella.

Loretta said, "Okay," and with that, she smiled broadly and left us.

"I feel so much better," said Loretta.

"A game plan usually settles things down pretty good," I replied.

I've just poured a cup of the hazelnut for Loretta when breakfast arrives, bland oatmeal, tea, wheat bread, and a fruit cup. Let the feast begin. I stay with her until she finishes the breakfast, then I head for

Home Depot to pick up some supplies to start the conversion from guest room to nursery.

I spend the morning rough drafting the work that I will do in the nursery. The work that must be done is extensive—new ceilings, walls, floors, closet, and that's just the structural stuff. This though, is a labor of love like no other. I run some other errands before visiting the gym for a workout. Pulling into the parking lot, I see my buddy Will's Buick. I'm glad because I haven't seen him since before Christmas. He went to North Carolina to spend the holidays with his parents. Though we've spoken on the telephone, we have not had a face to face or a meal. I change in the locker room and head up to the equipment floor. After getting off of the elevator, I see Will walking the treadmill.

I walk down and get on the treadmill beside him.

"Sup, bruh, how's the lady?" Will says.

I relate the morning's events to bring him up to date. I tell him about the nursery project.

Will replies, "Well, you know me, Vonstone, I'll just pay somebody."

We both laugh because my friend is *not* handy. We complete the workout laughing and talking all the way. Sometimes, I think we do more talking than anything else, but it's therapy for us both.

Will says, "You got time for a meal?"

"I've got to take a rain check brother. I need to make it back to the hospital for shift change."

"Shift change? Oh, parking."

My friend is a twenty-two-year veteran of the FDNY, and is intimately familiar with the tribulation of shift parking.

"Be sure you get plenty of sleep, bruh; I know that the missus needs you, but in all that running around, make sure that you take care of *you*, you hear, he admonishes?

"Good looking out, bruh," I respond. "You're off tomorrow, right, that means you're here early?" I ask.

"Yeah, let's have lunch," Will replies.

"Cool," I say. We walk out of the gym together to the parking lot, and say goodbye.

I stop off on the way back to the hospital and pick up some soup for Loretta and me to share because I just know that she would not have eaten much of the hospital dinner. She's sleeping when I arrive so I slip in and sit down noiselessly. I start off checking some emails before dozing off. I awake to her night nurse entering the room and snatching back the curtain. Loretta is awake and looking at me.

"You look tired," she says.

"Just a little," I say. The nurse is preparing to administer her meds. Apparently, the doctors are starting the magnesium sulfate drip this evening in advance of the Thursday cerclage procedure. In addition, one of the unfortunate effects of Trendelenburg is that it interferes with the normal movement of solid waste through the colon, so the stool often becomes impacted; therefore, the doctor has added a stool softener to the regimen for Loretta.

She relishes the soup, eating most of it; I was sorry not to have bought two, but I'm glad to see her put it away. We chat about this and that, and I catch her up on what's happening in the world. She is becoming acclimated to the rhythms and routines of her temporary home. She is able to tell me with remarkable detail the whys and wherefores of each shift.

"When I leave tonight, I think I'm going to walk down to the NICU and see what it is like down there," I say.

"Why?" asks Loretta.

"Just want to get a sense of the place I guess."

"Hey, guess what, I found a way in that doesn't involve walking all the way around the building in the freezing cold."

"Seriously, how?"

"I enter and exit through the ER."

"And they allow you to come in?" she asks.

"I imagine that the guards are accustomed to seeing me," I reply.

"Is there any word on the time of the procedure?" Loretta inquires.

"I spoke with Dr. Velella this afternoon, and she says that it will depend on the availability of an anesthesiologist, but it will not happen before 2:00 p.m."

"Don't come here too early because it will mean a really long day for you," says Loretta always looking out.

"Will it be any longer than your day?" I ask.

"Probably not, right?"

"Just let me be where I need to be please, ma'am," I tell her smiling.

Loretta smiles and squeezes my hand. I don't bother sharing that I will be staying with her on Thursday night, preferring to keep that bit of information for a surprise.

"I heard from one of the nurses that after the procedure, you'll be going to a new room on the fourth floor," I tell her. "I understand that it's very nice up there, a newly renovated private room."

"Nice," says Loretta. "The change will be good."

We alternately chat and sit quietly for the next hour and a half until Loretta dozes off. I kiss her, and she smiles in her sleep as I slip silently from the room and head down to explore the NICU floor before heading out through the ER.

CHAPTER 4

TUNA FISH SANDWICH

Lunch with Will was a keen distraction from everything that had been occupying my mind in the few weeks past. We both had different cuts of medium steak, greens and sweet potato, washing it all down with a large stein of German beer. We parted in the steakhouse parking lot, and I headed back to Flatbush to pick up Ma'Dear. I never get tired of back-roading it across Brooklyn, never touching a single main road except to cross it. As I round the corner, I see that Ma'Dear is waiting for me on the porch. Ma'Dear comes down to the driveway, and I rush round to open the door for her.

"Hello, Ma'Dear," I say as I bear hug her.

"Hello, son. How is Ms. Loretta?" she asks.

"Well, I guess you'll find out for yourself soon enough, ma'am. I promised Pop that I'd call while we're at the hospital so that he can say hello."

"How do you manage with parking around the hospital?" Ma'Dear asks.

"Usually, I arrive at the morning or the evening shift change, so I'm usually able to find a spot pretty easily, but because we're hear so early today, we'll have to go into the parking lot."

We find what appears to be the only remaining parking space in the entire garage and catch the elevator to the street level. Arriving at the hospital, we make our way to Loretta's room. She's surprised to see Ma'Dear.

43

"Hi, Mom," she says.

"Hello, my dear; how are you feeling?" says mother.

"Dad says to give you a kiss."

She leans over and gives Loretta a kiss on the head. As they chat I slip next door, into the hospitality room, to make three cups of herbal tea from a supply of Loretta's favorite teas that I brought with me. We three enjoy the tea and the company chatting about Ma'Dear's days as a patient care aide. She really has the temperament for taking care of people and has taken care of many over the years. We sip and chat away about an hour and a half with stories from mom about her patient care days. I remember to call up Pop for his moment in the sun. For whatever reason, Pop only visits on Sundays.

"Oh, I almost forgot," says Ma'Dear, "I brought you a prayer book for January."

She pulls a "Life Study Fellowship" prayer magazine from her bag and hands it to Loretta.

"Thanks, mom," says Loretta.

She has her own supply of reading material, but reading in *that* position makes her a bit nauseous. No doubt she appreciates the consideration. The nurse pops in to administer meds and to announce that visiting hours are over. Of course, that is more for the guest than for me because *my* visiting hours are never *really* over. We acknowledge the messenger and tell her that we'd be leaving shortly. Ma'Dear offers Loretta one of her Word Jumble books, which she's never without, but Loretta declines politely without explanation.

"We're going to leave you now, honey," I say.

"Thanks, this was a pleasant surprise and a lovely visit," she says looking at mother.

"Johnny and I will visit on Sunday if that's okay," Ma'Dear says.

"I'll look forward to it mom," and looking over at me she says, "and don't even think about coming back here tonight to watch me sleep."

We all laugh, and I tell her that I'm going to get a good night's rest after putting in an hour in the nursery. Ma'Dear and I kiss our goodbyes and depart, leaving Loretta with the nurse, and I lead a happy, relieved Ma'Dear out of the hospital back to the car.

Thursday roars to life at seven o'clock, an hour after I should've been up. Apparently, my body needed the extra rest, probably because I didn't get to bed until one o'clock working in the nursery. Fresh coffee awaits me in the kitchen, and I cook up some eggs with bacon and enjoy a leisurely breakfast, the first in a long time. Since the year began everything has been a blur, so it feels great eating unhurriedly at the kitchen island while trolling the news wire on my laptop.

Parking is a problem, albeit an expected one, but there's something about a less than frenetic start to the morning that puts me in a patient, relaxed frame of mind. The PCT is just going in with fresh linens and a gown for Loretta when I get there.

"Good morning, Mr. Wolfe," she says cheerily.

"A pleasant good morning to you, young lady."

"Hey, old man," says Loretta even before I part the curtain.

"Hey, good morning. How's the world's oldest teenager?" I ask as she grins broadly.

"Did you rest well," she queried?

"Fine, I say, but more importantly, did *you* rest well?"

"I'm not pooping despite the stool softener," she said squirming a bit.

"I haven't missed the doctor, have I?" I ask.

Just then, the nurse walked in, so I repeat the question to her.

"The doctor is making rounds right now," she answers. "I think that there are new instructions in your chart regarding your cerclage today, but the doctor will discuss that with you."

"Have you had breakfast yet?" Loretta asks.

"Are you buying?" I quip. "I actually blew through six o'clock this morning, so I decided to slow down, have a little breakfast and coffee, and catch up on the news."

"What time did you go to bed?"

"About one o'clock," I say.

"I knew it," says Loretta. "If you're not going to listen to me, at least listen to Will, because we appear to be expressing the same concern. You're only supposed to work until 11:00 p.m. Why don't you bring in some help?" she asks.

"Thanks, honey, but the hardest part will be the new sheetrock ceiling, so I'll bring in help for that part of the project."

"I just don't want you to burn yourself out because we need you," she said.

I didn't answer, not because I didn't want to, but because the "we" made it immediate and real. I hear what she's saying, I really do, but much in the same way that Lorraine had offered to carry the weight for her sister, and Loretta felt that this is something that she *could do*, indeed *must do*, this is my *must do*.

There's a knock, knock, knock at the door, and Loretta bids the visitor come in. It's the attending physician, and he's come to tell us that the procedure has been scheduled for 3:00 p.m. We look at each other, and I see relief in Loretta's eyes. This is yet another step that we can take to safeguard the kernel of hope protected inside her.

"Thank you, doctor, that is really good news," says Loretta.

Of course, we know that in hospital-speak, 3:00 p.m. probably means something on the order of 5:00 p.m., but we roll with it. The doctor is still there talking when the breakfast tray parts the curtains. Oatmeal, toast, and coffee with a banana appears to be the order of the day. The young lady kindly asks if I needed a tray, and I decline in favor of a cup of coffee in the hospitality room next door.

"Can I make you a cup of tea honey?" I inquire.

"Thanks, Earl Grey, please," she says smiling.

"Right away, ma'am," as I retrieve two teabags from the draw and nip next door to make the beverages.

As the midday hour approaches, Loretta and I make a bet as to whether transportation would be in to take her downstairs for the procedure *on time*. Neither of us believed that the timetable would hold up. Loretta said, "I think somebody will come in and tell us they've rescheduled for five o'clock, what do you think?"

"I think that if they have to push it to five, they'll likely postpone it for tomorrow. Perhaps four, I think."

About ten minutes later, Dr. Velella called to say that there was a confluence of all the necessary resources at the three o'clock hour.

So, perhaps, this was a good omen in that things were happening the way that they were supposed to; we could only hope that this was so.

About twenty minutes after my conversation with Dr. Velella, I walked down to the nurses station, (I swear they must be sick of me), to get some information on the post-surgery move to the fourth floor. Loretta and I decided that a strategy would be necessary due to the fact that she'd be here for the duration of the pregnancy. I came to a decision after watching the staff reaction to patients and family members, as well as their demeanor in all situations related to patient requests. The inescapable conclusion at which I arrived was that every person wearing a nurse's uniform was not meant to be a nurse, but came to that vocation for a variety of reasons other than being *called* to serve.

Therefore, since she would in effect be living on one floor or another in the maternity ward, I developed a strategy to navigate the minefield of the uncalled. Loretta, being the patient, would make all requests of the nursing staff. Any request that had to be repeated, or for which she waited for an unreasonable amount of time regardless to who it was made, would come from me. I would necessarily be the hammer to deliver repeat requests complaints and rapid escalations, and not always in the most diplomatic way. The staff did not like my way, but they responded to it by doing what was needed without repetition being necessary.

It is a method that I've developed over time in response to people in the service sector testing the fences. They do this to determine how far and how fast they can move you down their hierarchy if priorities. In their defense, their evaluation is often done in response to limited or diminishing resources, and though I am sometimes tempted to be sympathetic to the situation, I had to temper my compassion with the substantial needs of my wife. Loretta would often apologize for me, and the staff would feel sorry for her, being married to such an unreasoning asshole, but she'd *always* get the things that she needed, and then some. Eventually, I had to become *that guy* less and less as the staff became accustomed to the level of service below, which I (we) would not permit them to slip.

At about ten after three transportation came for Loretta, not bad timing, all things considered. They verified her identity from her chart, moved her over to the transport bed and, wheeled her down to the elevator. When we got to the pre-op area, we realized that there was going to be a bit of a wait while they prepped the OR. A charming Mennonite nurse candidate named Rachel came over with a scrub suit clad man, who identified himself as the anesthesiologist, in tow. He explained that he would be applying the previously elected spinal tap, as well as what to expect.

The doctor excused himself to return to the OR and prepare, leaving Rachel to chat with us for a while. She would periodically disappear into the back to keep us abreast of the gradual preparedness of the operating theatre as well as the arrival of the various actors. The nurses came out and wheeled Loretta into the OR, tearing her hand from mine as they went. I told Loretta that I'd be running upstairs quickly to check on her new accommodations, but I'd be right here during the procedure and here when they bring her out.

Technology is wonderful, especially the tech that can be directed to your specific need, to address your specific problem. The cerclage and ancillary procedures are the perfect example. Doctors identify a problem, in this case, an incompetent cervix. They then determine that because the uterus begins to funnel, they'll need to take a series of actions in order to keep the pregnancy viable. So they carefully stitch the cervix, place the patient in Trendelenburg in order to minimize the pressure on the funneling uterus, and begin the administration of a series of drugs to keep the uterus quiet. I love freakin' science!

I walk up to Loretta's room on the second floor, but when I get inside the room, I notice that it is devoid of her things. Just then, a well-groomed gentleman with amazingly quaffed hair, wearing a uniform bearing the hospital logo, entered the room.

"Good afternoon, sir," he said greeting me warmly.

I almost feel as if I know him.

"A good afternoon to you as well, sir," I replied.

I identify the accent immediately as emanating from Trinidad & Tobago.

"We've already moved your wife to her new room, but not to worry, we wheeled everything down as is. We did not touch her things, with the exception of the phone charger. Folks always forget their phone charger," he reported.

"Thanks for that," I replied.

"I just came back to give a last look round before heading back up," he said. "May I show you where it is?"

"Thanks, I'd appreciate that very much," I replied.

"By the way, my name is Andrew," he said introducing himself.

"I'm Vonstone," I replied shaking his hand enthusiastically,

"Could your wife use a small refrigerator in her room? The hospital offers them as a courtesy to long-term patients."

"Yes, that would be outstanding, Andrew. Thank you."

"No problem, I'll bring it up later."

This newly renovated wing of the hospital is a stark and welcomed departure from the décor of the previous digs. There was abundant wood paneling everywhere and matching furniture. The paint on the walls is a very complimentary peach to the walnut finish. I tell Andrew that I think that my wife will be very comfortable in this wing, and I think I will as well since I'll be spending quite a few nights here.

"You're a good man," he says. "Most fellows would be visiting the girlfriend."

"Not me, friend, I *know* where I need to be," I reply emphatically.

Andrew smiles and says he'll be back with the fridge later. I thank him again, take a last look around, and head back down to the OR to stand watch. On my way down, I pass the nurses station and introduce myself and tell them that my wife is currently in surgery, but would shortly be delivered into their care. "We're expecting her, Mr. Wolfe, and everything will be ready for her when she arrives," said the nurse. "And I don't know if anyone has told you, but you are welcome to stay with her in the room."

"Yes, thank you, I've been made aware. As a matter of fact, I'll be staying with her tonight," I say.

I tell the nurse that I'll be returning to the OR and head for the elevator. I pass the hospitality room where there are some fresh sandwiches on the counter. Remembering that Loretta will likely be hungry, I zoom across the street quickly, to a restaurant, which has the distinction of being the only game in town, where I procure some hot lentil soup to go with one of the sandwiches upstairs. Arriving back at the OR, Rachel remarks, that it's good that I bought food because she'll likely be hungry, and any waiting dinner will be an hour cold by the time she gets to it.

"What did you get her, may I ask?"

"Lentil soup and a sandwich," I tell her.

"Good, what will you eat?" Rachel asks?

"A hospital tuna fish sandwich," I reply.

"They're pretty good, aren't they?" says Rachel.

"Yes, I know, I like them. How much longer do you think Rachel?"

"Let me check for you, okay?"

As Rachel is moving toward the door, we notice Dr. Velella coming out. She takes one look at the bag next to me and says, "Hot food, good, she'll be hungry, something pretty light?"

"Lentil soup and a sandwich," I reply.

Dr. Velella offers a full briefing on the procedure. She says that it went very well, and all that remains is to implement the other aspects of the retention protocol and hope for the best. She assures me that she'll be following up daily even if we do not see her at the hospital, but offers me her cell phone number in the event that we need her or have any questions. They wheel Loretta out as we're chatting.

"Hey, trooper," I say to her. "You look terrific"!

"Oh shut up. Tell me that's hot soup in that bag," she says.

"That's hot soup in the bag. I knew you'd be a bit peckish," I tell her.

As I walk beside the bed, she says, "Peckish? I'm starving."

"I think that you'll like the room," I tell her it has a much homier feel than your last room."

"Are you tired?" she asks me.

"Oh just a bit," I say, "but I'm planning on having my best night's rest since you've been in here."

As we exit the elevator on the fourth floor, who should we encounter but Andrew with Loretta's fridge on a cart.

"I think we're headed in the same direction," says Andrew.

"I sincerely hope that you're right, Andrew," I reply.

Transportation wheels Loretta into her new room and gets her situated, while Andrew and I chat outside for the moment. After a few minutes, they exit the room, and we go in.

"Honey, meet Andrew TNT." I say, provoking laughter. "He was kind enough to secure a fridge for you."

"Thank you so much, Andrew," says Loretta.

"This will make my stay her so much more pleasant."

"You are ever so welcome, ma'am," says Andrew. "If there is anything that I can ever do to help you, just ask for Andrew."

"We will, thank you again," I say.

As he leaves, I get a basin of hot water and tidy Loretta up in preparation for dinner. As hungry as she is, she would never wish to eat without tidying up, that much I know. Adjusting the bed for the meal, I get her dinner in front of her, and she starts to spoon it in hungrily. I smile and nip down to the hospitality room for a tuna fish sandwich and a cup of tea. After dinner, I slip into the bathroom, shower, and get ready for bed. Loretta smiles broadly as I emerge in pajamas and slippers with my clothes in a bag.

"You're staying with me tonight?" she asks me.

"Well, I told you that I was going to enjoy my first decent night's rest since you've been in here," I tell her returning the smile.

CHAPTER 5

THE STORM

The new room is quite homey, and we both take to the new environment. I don't know whether it's the fake woodwork, or the nice bathroom with shower, but this room has a completely different feel to it. The whole floor has a different feel to it, including the nurse's station. They don't seem to have that "what the hell does he want look about them, well not yet anyway." The only problem that I see is that the floors look a bit grubby. I don't think that Loretta has noticed yet, but she will soon enough. I think that they only mop and clean the rooms on certain days, so I make a mental note to tell someone about it.

I pass an unusual night in the hospital with frequent interruptions as the PCT keeps coming in to do vitals. I think that Loretta is quite accustomed to the interruptions, and I suppose that I would be too if I had to deal with it nightly. I leave after Dr. Kelly makes his rounds. He never stays long and doesn't have any information to share, but he is the gynecologist of record. On my way past the nurse's station, I mention the floor and ask how often they clean the room. They say that this is supposed to happen daily, which is a bit of a surprise to me. No matter, I know what I have to do.

The fridge is a godsend, because not only are we able to store hospital goodies, but even more important, some of Loretta's favorites from home. She loves my soups and stews, so I try to have some on hand for her to replace a hospital meal or two. If all else fails, I have the place on the corner for a standby for a quick meal. I stop at Home Depot on the way home to pick up a bucket of compound and a few other supplies. Arriving home, I do a quick change, eat breakfast, check some emails, and settle in for a good six hours of work in the nursery. The days are starting to blend one into the other. Typically, days are defined by the activities that are assigned to them. But since my days are taken up with hospital, gym, and construction, all the days have taken on a sameness that puts me in a bit of a fog sometimes.

Sometimes at shift change, departing staff will try to give a parking space to someone coming on. This usually works only if the arriving shift mate gets there early enough to be waiting when the other comes out. Technically, if your shift mate is already outside of the building and you're waiting for their spot, you're already late. Well, that being said, when I get to the hospital, I observe exhaust fumes rising from between two cars, and observe a driver behind the wheel.

"Excellent," I say to myself, "a spot."

I pull up ant wait behind the driver, which will allow her to exit the parking space unimpeded, after which I would pull up and parallel park.

Well, after ten minutes, another car pulls in front of the parked car and puts on their right indicator, signaling their intention to park in the spot for which I have been waiting for ten minutes. The three of us sit and wait for another few minutes, until the arriving driver exits her car and exchanges words with the parked driver. After the word exchange, she makes her way back to me.

"That's my spot," she said. "He's been holding it for me."

"I'm so sorry," I replied. "I had absolutely no idea, and perhaps if I had not been waiting here for almost fifteen minutes, that might actually mean something, but since I have been waiting here for fifteen minutes, I think I'll be parking there today."

"He's not going to let you in," she said.

"Has all night, has he, or you for that matter?" I said, "Because I do. He will leave, and when he does, I will pull in, and you will go find another parking spot."

Forty five seconds later, I was walking across the street to the hospital, and the interloper had made a U-turn and gave me a "have a nice day" finger gesture. I smile and keep on truckin'.

Trendelenburg is wearing on Loretta. I see it in her face as I enter the room. She smiles and says, "Have you eaten?"

"No, I thought I'd come here so you could buy dinner. What'd they bring?" It's over there, please don't open it. It smells absolutely awful."

"I'll take it out, and warm up what I brought you." Her face lights up. I take the tray out and go down to the hospitality room to warm up dinner.

"Here you are my dear, one square for you, and one square for me."

"Lasagna," she says, "Bless you."

"Spinach lasagna," I reply. I raise the bed and set it before her and she dives in.

"I brought extra for the fridge, perhaps lunch or dinner tomorrow."

"What's in the other bag?" said Loretta eyeing the other package.

"I bought a swifter cleaning system this afternoon to get this place tidied up a bit." I tell her.

"When I asked this morning about the cleaning schedule, the answer that I got didn't make sense, so I took steps." She just smiles and keeps eating her homemade spinach lasagna. After dinner, I give the room a good going over, and we both feel much better. Our first post-cleaning visitor is a PCT who remarks on the *clean fresh smell.* Loretta smiles and tells her that I just finished dusting and cleaning the room and bathroom. After that, I guess that the word got around, because there were a steady stream of *drop-ins* for no apparent reason.

I realize that I can't tell them to stop using the nasty mop and bucket. But if I make it really obvious to them that I'm cleaning after their custodial staff, I can start a conversation where I can express our displeasure with the nasty mop bucket. The patient representative, a nice lady whom we had met previously, drops in to ask if we're satisfied with the room as well as to drop off some previously promised information. She immediately notices something different.

"My goodness, what is that delightful smell?"

"It's called Zoflora," I tell her.

I explain the presence of this foreign smell and why I'm using it.

"I am not at all comfortable with how the mopping is done. The custodial staff seems to move from room to room with the same dirty mop and water, dragging contaminants along with them. It gets worse if they're also including the hallways."

"I see what you mean, but why didn't you call me, or tell the staff?" she asks.

"I'm pacing myself," I say with a smile.

Loretta, knowing my meaning, lets out a Trendelenburg laugh. The rep looks at me quizzically as I explain that I quickly gained the reputation of being a fierce and vocal advocate for all things Loretta.

"Oh, a troublemaker," she says.

"Quite, and unapologetically so, I might add," I say.

"That is exactly what you're supposed to do, that's your job here, and from what I hear, you're good at it," says the advocate.

"I try to take all the bad feelings with me when I leave the ward each day, so that none of it remains with Loretta," I explain. "So I have resolved to start slowly and pick the battles."

Listening to the radio on the way home, I hear reports of a snow front moving steadily our way, and it appears to be holding together pretty well. They always *say* we might get hit big-time, but it's almost always a near miss or not as bad as forecasted. I get set up in the nursery and start to work, but then the phone starts. Everyone is calling for updates, and wanting to know if it's okay to visit. After the third phone call, I hit the showers and await the fourth.

Overnight, the weather forecast becomes more concrete, and it becomes obvious that a major snow system is in our very near future. I decide to get an early start and get some food supplies, water, and rock salt into the house. After packing away the groceries, I lay down a heavy layer of salt on the drive and walkways—packing a bag, and head for the gym to get a quick workout and steam, before heading back to the hospital for my shift. Fortunately, the parking gods favor me, and there is an interloper-free spot waiting for me. I arrive on the fourth floor just in time to see a member of the janitorial crew rolling his cleaning cart, with attached mop bucket, up to the nursing station.

"Don't you usually *start* at the other end of the hall?" asks one of the nurses.

"Yes, but today, I was told to start at 243," he says.

"I don't know why." I smile to myself as I pass.

"I do," says the nurse.

And I imagine her motioning in my direction as I pass by the station.

"So much for pacing myself," I say chuckling.

The cleaner follows me into the room, and Loretta is out of bed, cleaned up, changed, and fresh linens being put on.

"Mawnin', ma'am," I say. "And how are you today?"

"Did you hear about the snow that's coming later? Are you leaving early for home?" she says sounding super concerned?

"No, I brought a bag, so I'm staying right here with you," I assure her.

She doesn't reply, but smiles and looks relieved.

The snow started slowly about dinnertime, but you knew that this was serious because it was wicked cold. The wind had picked up as well and it started to stick on hard surfaces immediately. A thought entered my mind immediately, and I shared it with Loretta.

"You know, I'm thinking that I should have taken the bus over."

"Why?"

"If this gets bad, as they're now predicting, I may not be able to move the car," I answer. "I should've taken the bus over. If the car is snowed in, I'll have to take the bus anyway."

We chat for a few minutes about this and that, and all the time, I'm thinking that I have a snow Brush in the trunk, and I should go downstairs, brush off the car, drive it home, and come back on the bus. Dinner arrives and I position Loretta for her meal and go get tea and a tuna sandwich for myself. By the time we're done with dinner and chit chatting with staff coming and going, there are two inches on the ground, and it's coming harder than ever. Clearly, nobody's going anywhere.

The blanket of snow always makes everything look so clean and uniformed, muffling all the sounds, and keeping the heavy traffic off the streets. It's almost comforting to look out on the streets with all the cars covered for the night in blankets of snow. Standing at the window looking out at the scene of tranquility sets one's spirit at ease until the quiet is broken by a barging PCT. As that thought passed through my head, the door opens and light from the hall pierces the scene of tranquility.

"Sorry," says the interrupting PCT.

"It's okay," I half whisper. "Come on in."

She comes in and goes directly for the bedpan as Loretta stirs awake, again.

"What's it doing out there?" she asks.

"Coming hard," I reply. "Still coming hard."

I'm so glad I'm here I think to myself, sitting down in the recliner by the window. I awaken with every visitation but have a surprisingly decent nights rest.

"I feel bad that you're not home getting a better night's rest in bed," says Loretta almost scolding me.

"I'm right where I need to be ma'am, thank you very much," I shoot back. "I suspect that the morning shift will bring us some staffing surprises, so I think my being here is a good thing."

"I've been thinking, I don't have a snow shovel in the car. so I won't be able to dig out once it stops."

What was I thinking? I have sand and salt, but no shovel.

It's still pretty early, but the shift change should be in full swing. The hallway is deathly silent, and I suspect that there will be some staffing shortages this morning, but for now, it's just us in the early morning hours chatting away. I get up and head into the bathroom. I shower quickly and dress because there's much to do today, and it will all need to be accomplished by bus.

I get Loretta up, and she walks to the bathroom as I manage the trolley. Even with all the Colace, Loretta still has had minimum bowel movements. After about five minutes, I check on her and realize that she has been straining a bit. She knows instinctively that this was a mistake, but the gravity of Trendelenburg is having its way and she is in great discomfort.

"I think I may have done something," she says.

"Something like what," I ask.

"I don't know," she says. "I'm just feeling a little pressure in my lower abdomen."

"Let's get you back into the bed, and I'll call for the doctor to stop by," I tell her. "I'm sure it's nothing."

I get her back into the bed and properly repositioned, then I walk down to the nurse's station to speak with the charge nurse. About ten minutes later, the doctor comes into the room and after Loretta explains what took place, the doctor leaves the room to arrange for a precautionary ultrasound.

The ultrasound shows s little advance in the funneling; nothing alarming, but this accounts for the pressure that she's feeling. And this new pressure is likely the result of the mild straining on the toilet. Loretta feels a little guilty for the momentary lapse and says, "I am never doing that again."

I don't add to the guilt with any words at all. Even words of comfort or reassurance, at this point, may not help.

I leave the hospital after breakfast, and make my way to where the car is parked. It is buried under mounds of snow, which is still falling, and in addition, the ploughs have begun to do their work, and I'm completely sealed in. Once this turns to ice, I'm done for a couple of days at a minimum. *Well, at least the buses are still running,* I say to myself as I spot one approaching in the distance. I walk over to the bus stop and wait for my ride.

My street is completely inundated with snow. Some of the neighbors, the smart ones, are out keeping up with the snowfall. Living in New York, you learn that big snowfalls should be taken in small bites. You go out every few hours and keep the amount that's on the ground manageable. The pulverized rock salt that I put down yesterday has had a meaningful effect so there isn't much hard shoveling to do; it's mostly slush that I push away and apply some more salt.

My phone rings, and it's Loretta. "How's the house?" she asks. "Is there a lot of shoveling to do?"

"No, the pulverized salt worked remarkably well. I'm so glad I put in the extra work." I knew where this was going.

"I hope you're going to stay home tonight," she says.

"Geez, okay, so you're tired of me. I'll stay home tonight."

"You know that's not what I mean, sir," says Loretta. "I just feel bad that you're sleeping on this cot when there's a perfectly good king size bed at home sitting empty."

"Okay, if it will make you feel better, I'll sleep at home tonight." I spend the day inside working in the nursery as well as catching up on a multitude of emails and returning phone calls. The snow abates at some point in the late afternoon, leaving Brooklyn under a quiet sheet of white. I pause from my labors in the nursery to enjoy a cup of coffee while gazing out of one of the windows in the nursery into the back yard. I can't help but muse about the future occupant, and how many times he will gaze out upon this vista.

The ceiling is up, and I know that I promised Loretta that I would bring in help to get it done, but this is a labor that I do not wish to share. I'm happy as I step back and gaze upon it. It's absolutely perfect. My cousin, Hazzie, who I learned sheetrock and taping from, would be proud. An unusual wave of tiredness begins to move over me. It almost feels drug induced the way it falls like a curtain until I remember that my day started quite early, and involved much physically taxing activity. Will's voice echoes in my ears, "You can't forget to take care of you, bruh."

With those words ringing in my head, I make my way into the shower, then collapse into a deep winter's night sleep. I don't call to say good night; I'm just too bushed, so I whisper it onto the back of a cold north bound wind, and send it her way.

I call Loretta bright and early (because I know she's probably up anyway), and she shares the details of the evening with me.

"I'm bringing breakfast, so please be sure not to partake in the hospital's offering," I tell her.

"Food from home, thank you," she replies.

After a good hot shower, I pack a bag, including breakfast for two, grab my sturdiest snow shovel, and head down to the bus stop. I tell myself that if a cab happens by, I'll flag it down, but I'm not hopeful. Cabs are at an absolute premium when it snows, and besides, the bus gives me virtual door-to-door service, so what more could I ask for? After waiting at the bus stop for ten minutes with no bus in sight, I decide to start walking the bus route instead of standing around in the snow.

Walking in the early morning cold is quite bracing and leaves me alone with my thoughts. I thought of what my son will be or be come. Will he like me, and will I be a good dad? I have to remember to ask my dad if any of these questions crossed his mind as I was pending. I turn to look back on the bus route to see if there is any sign of a bus—there is no sign as far as my eye can see. and I'm already about a mile and a half into my three and a half mile trek. My phone is ringing somewhere inside the padding.

"Hello?"

"Hey, chef, where's my breakfast?" asks the patient.

"I beg your indulgence, ma'am, but I'm on foot this morning. The bus route is completely absent of buses, and of course, taxis are not to be found."

"*You're walking??!!*" Loretta asks sounding quite alarmed.

"Yes," I reply. "My feet work quite well, and there is no reasonable option here."

"Aren't you cold?" she asks.

"Not even a little bit. I'm just walking and thinking," I tell her.

"About what?" she asks.

"Our son, and if he's going to like me, and if I'm going to be a good dad," I reply.

"The big questions, huh?" she comments.

"The biggest," I say. "Do you ever ask yourself these questions?"

"I seem to be thinking about them more and more," I offer.

"No, it never occurred to me at all, I must confess," says Loretta. "And I don't think that it was important to Doreen Alexander (Loretta's mom) either, that any of her children *like* her."

"Yeah, I know. I think I need to rest for a bit," I tell her. "Walking on un-cleared sidewalks is quite tiring."

"You're crazy," she says.

"Maybe," I say.

I approach a coffee shop on the corner of McDonald Av. and Cortelyou Rd. This place is always open, and I pray it's open this morning. The sidewalk in front is clear, which is a good sign. There are lights and the kitchen exhaust on the side of the building is blowing the smell of bacon onto the street. The counterman gives me a queer look as I walk in with my bag and shovel.

"You're buried somewhere, huh?" he asks.

"Yeah, and then some," I reply.

"What can I get you?" he asks.

"Just coffee, thanks."

He comes back with a mug of piping hot coffee. I ignore the handle and wrap my hands around the mug, and it feels so good.

"Where's your car?" he asks planting a cup o'Joe in front of me.

Without asking, he puts a small plate with two slices of bacon in front of me, with a smile.

"On the house," he says.

"I'm in front of the hospital," I tell him. "I was waiting for the twenty-three, but it wasn't happening, so I started walking."

"That was smart; you'd probably still be there because I've only seen one bus all morning, and you're my first customer," he explains.

"What time do you open?" I ask.

"I get here at five and open at six," he replies, offering me more bacon with a glance at the grill. I politely decline with a hand gesture.

"I'm glad I didn't wait, if that's the case."

"More coffee?"

"No, thanks, I should get moving," I tell him.

Feeling sufficiently recovered, I pay the check and leave the diner. Back on the street, there's still no bus, so I resolve to just walk the remaining eleven blocks to the hospital.

I turn the corner a few blocks later, and the hospital is in sight at the top of the hill, so feeling energized, I plow through the last few blocks and reach Ft. Hamilton Pkwy where the car is parked across from the hospital. I pop the trunk and manage to open it enough to slide the shovel inside. Making my way in through the ER entrance, I am greeted by a succession of tired faces who are obviously remnants of a shift change that never quite materialized. Loretta is surprised to see me when I walked in.

"Wow, you made it pretty quickly. Didn't you bother to stop and rest?" she asks.

"I stopped at the diner at McDonald Av. for a cup of coffee," I reply. "I rested for about ten minutes and then pressed on. Are you hungry, ma'am?"

"Starving," she says.

"I have everything all set. Let me get it warmed up and we'll eat," I tell her as I scoot over to the hospitality room to warm it up and make the tea.

CHAPTER 6

VISITATION

Breakfast was an unqualified hit, as the usual cast of characters, nurses and PCT's and a patient or two, floated in and out, all commenting on the delicious breakfast smell emanating from the room. As we finish up breakfast, Dr. Kelly walks in and of course comments on the fact that this does not smell like a hospital breakfast.

"And how are we doing today?" he asks.

"Great, now that I've started the day with a home cooked breakfast," says Loretta smiling a bacon smile.

"I know exactly what you mean. I had a rather ambitious breakfast this morning myself," says Dr. Kelly with an unusually personal retort.

"Have you been having at least one significant bowel movement daily?" he asks.

"No, not at all," says Loretta, almost grimacing.

"Sounds like someone needs *a mess o' greens*," I say.

Kelly laughs and says, "Now that might help a lot."

So I guess I have my next assignment, maybe for dinner tomorrow. I'm thinking maybe some nice slippery okra.

"Are you still experiencing pressure?" he asks.

"Yes, steady pressure," says Loretta.

"Is it any more intense than before, or about the same?" he asks.

"Just about the same, she says," looking over at me.

"Well, I don't know," I say jokingly.

63

"If I feel it, you usually know about it," she says correctly.

Loretta quite properly shares all of these details with me, so I serve as a reliable repository of all things associated with the pregnancy.

"It may feel uncomfortable, but no real harm will come from not going for a while. You are having *some* movement right?" asks the doctor.

"Yes, a few pieces about every other day or so," replies Loretta.

"That's not too bad at all," he says. "I'll check on you on Monday, okay?"

"Okay, Dr. Kelly," says Loretta with a slight smile.

Dr. Kelly departs, and Loretta suddenly looks a bit sleepy.

"Are you sleepy, ma'am?" I ask.

"Yeah, does it show," she asks.

"I think we could both use a nap."

And with that, I settle into the recliner for a late morning nap.

I go down and begin the process of digging out the car about mid-afternoon. The process is back breaking because I have to uncover the car and dig a path to drive out. All snow ploughs push to the right, so if one comes by, I'll be sealed in once again unless I can dig it out before it freezes. When I'm almost finished, I see a young lady standing on the sidewalk, arms folded against the cold. After I finish, she approaches, greets me, and asks to borrow my shovel. I recognized her on approach as the young "*lady*" who had choice gestures for me when I didn't surrender my parking space to her.

The universe indeed has a perverse sense of humor. She recognizes me mid-sentence but presses on with only a brief pause.

"Good afternoon, sir," she says. "Would it be possible for me to ..." suddenly pausing uncomfortably?

"Please go on," I say suppressing a smile.

" ... ah to borrow your shovel when you're done with it?" she asks almost sheepishly.

I so believe in the " ... *heaping coals of fire thing.*"

"Of course, it would be impolite and un-neighborly of me to refuse you," I tell her. "Is this not how neighbors behave toward one another?" I chide.

"Shit. I'd rather leave that thing buried till spring," she says.

"As opposed to what," I reply. After a long pause I say, "We create our own situations, don't we? Good luck!"

I shake my head as I put the shovel into the trunk and walk away. I would've helped her dig out even without the apology, but she felt that it was hanging over her head, and that was apparently too much for her to bear.

Loretta had to beg be to stop talking, she was laughing so hard. "I would've dug her out," I tell her.

"I know you would have," says Loretta. If she had either shut up, apologized, or merely acknowledged the prior encounter, we could have both had a laugh about it. But she tried to brass it out, and that was unacceptable to me."

I'm pretty sweaty and in need of a shower, so I get my shaving kit, loungewear, a towel, and head for the bathroom. After my shower, I warm up some home cooked food for us and make some tea. The dinner is really good, if I do say so myself, but Loretta agrees. Sleep comes early and quickly after all my exertions in the tundra.

"Hey, you awake, you awake?" asks Loretta again.

"What, who, you okay, everything alright?" I ask somewhat excitedly.

"I'm fine, no emergency; I just awoke suddenly from a dream," she said rather ominously. "I know that you had some ideas on names for the baby, but we have to name him *Joshua,*" she said deliberately.

I had been thinking and meditating intently on names for our son, but her tone was such that I knew she has experienced something, so I did not question it.

"Now that's a name," I said, "definitely! How did you come up with it? What lead you there?" I asked.

I was interested to know about the dream that she had.

"Zzzzzzzzzz," is all that came back to me. Well, this should make one hell of a breakfast conversation in the morning. She woke just long enough to deliver a subconscious message and promptly went back to sleep. Great, now I'm wide-awake thinking about all this.

There was a time that I can remember when people operating, even fractionally outside the borders of functional normalcy were at best marginalized. Worst cases were relegated to the *Bedlams* and *Bellevues* of the world. Today, in this era of smart phones, smart cars, and smart every other damn thing, where there's an app for *that*, there seems to be a pill for every mania, malady, or psychosis. This renders those, who in a previous time, would have been inmates in some institution or the other, fully functioning members of society, with keys to the meds lockup and everything.

Do not misunderstand my meaning, these pharmaceutical advances and treatments are a wonderful thing. Moving people from the sidelines, and placing them in the mainstream of life with the mere administration of a pill, is nothing shy of miraculous. But like with any wonder cure, in order for the remedy to work, you've got to take it.

Early Sunday morning, like a reveille bugle, a nurse, we'll call her Susan, storms into the room, throws back the curtain noisily with one practiced motion, and begins to bark questions. Loretta looks at me and me back at her, then we both look at Susan, and back at each other. With that, Susan leaves the room in the same manner in which she came. But for the gently fluttering curtains, it was as if she was never there. Thinking it some bizarre shared nightmare, we both settled back into the briefest of early morning naps.

About an hour later, the door gently opens, and we're aware that someone is in the room.

"Good morning, Loretta," says an annoyingly chirpy little voice. It's Susan, and she's the very picture of pleasantness and bed-side manner.

"Good morning," we reply.

"I'm Susan, and I'll be your nurse until Wednesday morning," she says, writing her name on the board.

She goes on for another minute or so telling us that she came in at five to relieve our night nurse; and finishes up by assuring Loretta that it she needed anything at all, she'd be all over it. It was as if she'd never been in this room and spoken to us before. The *bizzaro world* moment having ended, Loretta and I look at each other and stifle a laugh.

"Meds?" I ask Loretta.

"Please don't start laughing, we cannot afford a laughing fit, but yeah definitely meds," she replies.

Neither one of us spoke a word while Susan was in the room. We simply looked back and forth between Susan and each other and nodded slowly when we thought she was done.

"Even if I was not already planning to hang around for the next couple of nights, I think that Susan has convinced me," I tell *Loretta* reassuringly. As we lay there chatting, we hear someone say, "Knock, knock."

We immediately recognize the voice as that of David Kelly.

As he walks in and sees me, he says, "It appears that you almost live here."

"What do you mean *almost?*" I reply. "I spend more time here than at home."

"Well, Loretta, how is the little fella doing today?" he asks.

"I think that he wants to come out, really soon?" she tells him.

I immediately turn and look at her because I'd not heard that this morning. I also realize that we had not discussed the unofficial midnight naming ceremony.

Loretta tells Dr. Kelly about the pain that she is experiencing.

"The pain is as if the urethral opening is straining against the stitches," she tells Dr. Kelly.

"I'm going to give Dr. Velella a call to see what her thoughts are on removing the stitches," he tells us as he peruses Loretta's chart. "You know what, I'm going to leave her service a message right now. You'll hear from me a bit later Loretta, okay?"

"Thanks, Dr. Kelly," says Loretta as Kelly walks out dialing Dr. Velella's service.

He looks a bit concerned as he pauses outside the door to initiate the message on the service. I don't convey any of this to Loretta and instead change the subject completely.

"Mom and dad are stopping by this afternoon at about two they say," I report.

Visitors break up the monotony in a big way and are always quite welcome.

"So, I've got to get spruced up for the occasion then," she says smiling.

Loretta picks at her lunch, and I put away a tuna fish sandwich, as I am not particularly hungry. We're grousing about the hospital food when my phone rings. It's Dr. Velella, and she has had a conversation with Dr. Kelly regarding the increasing pain at the cerclage site.

"Good afternoon, Mr. Wolfe, its Sandra Velella," she says. "Are you at the hospital right now?"

"Yes, I'm here with Loretta," I reply.

I put my phone on speaker and close the door.

"Very good, you're together. I had a talk with Dr. Kelly this afternoon regarding the pain that you're feeling. It sounds as if you're straining against the cerclage, and if that turns out to be the case, then the cerclage has done all its work and must now be removed. We talked at the beginning about this process being done in stages, with certain actions being performed at each stage. This is another stage in the process, and that is how we're approaching it. I'm scheduling you for some imaging in the morning just to be certain. It'll take some rearranging of the schedule in the morning, but we'll get it done, okay, Loretta?" she says.

"Thanks, Dr. Velella, I really appreciate it," replies Loretta.

"What does that imply for the overall pregnancy?" I inquire.

"Well, each stage in the process is meant to buy us time, to keep him inside and growing in his ideal environment. The cerclage is a bridge procedure, meant to do the work of a normal cervix, at least for a while. The next stage will involve continuing the magnesium sulfate drip to help quiet the womb and slow down the process still more. This will be done for the remainder of your pregnancy. But the most important step is the steroid injections for the baby's lung development. After we remove the cerclage, things *may* begin to progress more quickly, and the lungs are critical for any premature birth, so we must inject the steroid to give him every chance."

The words sat there for a good while because we all knew that we were at a critical point in the pregnancy. Finally, Loretta said, "We'll do whatever we have to give him every chance to join us in the world.

"By the way," I said not wanting to let this perfect segue slip away, "I've been meaning to get back here all morning, and this seems like the perfect time. Where did you come up with Joshua? It seems to have come out of the blue."

"What do you mean?" said Loretta.

"I was afraid of this," I said almost laughing.

"On that note," said Dr. Velella, "I'll be ringing off now; much to do before tomorrow. You'll be hearing from me before six o'clock, okay?"

"Thanks, Dr. Velella," says Loretta rather cheerfully as she ends the call and turns to face me.

"Now then," I say, "you woke me in the middle of the night and made sure that I was awake and listening. After making certain that I was lucid, you told me that we had to name our baby, Joshua. I was certain that it was some kind of prophetic dream because after I agreed to the dreamscape naming, I questioned you on its genesis, all I received were snores in response."

"Why didn't you say anything before now because this is a little freaky?" asks Loretta sounding intrigued.

"One thing after the other this morning, and I almost felt as if I dreamt it, except for the fact that I could not get back to sleep once you left me with that."

"Wow, I definitely wouldn't have been able to get back after that bit," she replies.

"Be thankful then, that it did not drop on you ma'am," I retort.

"Joshua," she says test-driving the name. "Joshua Wolfe."

"That's a name," I say.

We both say it again together, almost wistfully, then look at each other and laugh.

"Did I miss something?" says a voice at the door.

The familiar voice is that of Debbie Marshall, one of the Debbie(s) from Loretta's church. "You may have to tell that one again."

"Debbie, what a surprise. It's so good to see you," says Loretta.

"Hey, Debbie, good to see you, ma'am."

"Hey, guys, I wanted to come sooner, but the snow held me back," said Debbie.

"I know," says Loretta. "Von walked from home yesterday because there were no buses or taxis."

"No, you're kidding, right?" asks Debbie.

"I started walking when I got tired of standing in the snow at the bus stop. I stopped at a coffee shop to warm up with a hot beverage; still no bus or taxi. Before you know it, I was within sight of the hospital, and the bus or taxi was academic at that point," I explain.

"I'm impressed," says Debbie.

"What is that exquisite aroma emanating from your bag, my dear?" I ask inquisitively?

"I was wondering the same thing," says Loretta. "Whatever it is has my mouth watering.

"Oh, sorry, I forgot that I brought you lunch. Nothing special, just a little dahl and rice with some spinach," she said.

"Thank you so much, Debbie. I've been dying for a little dahl and rice. That was so thoughtful of you to do."

Debbie smiled broadly and said, "It's only a little dahl, Loretta, no big deal, but I'm happy that you appreciate it."

"I'll get some plates, ladies," I said.

"I brought plates from home," says Debbie.

With that, Debbie stands up and begins to unpack the shopping bag.

"Okay then, tea, anyone?" I said, trying to make myself useful.

"Yes, thank you," says Debbie, as I rise to go make the tea.

When I return with the tea, they are both laughing hysterically. I give Loretta the wide-eye look with the head tilt, and she says, "I know, I know, but look," pointing at the table.

Upon the table Debbie has laid out lunch service stoneware with an oriental pattern. I smile at the touching gesture that she has made to cheer her friend.

"Debbie, I don't know what to say. The lunch was a lovely gesture, but this display is really touching. Thank you so much," says Loretta.

"I know that you're stuck in here and just wanted to do something nice for you," says Debbie.

"Wow, this was really something special," I say as I serve the tea.

"So, tell it again. Tell what I missed as I came through the door just now," says Debbie sounding thoroughly intrigued.

I proceed to tell of the midnight naming ceremony, and how Loretta has absolutely no memory of the details surrounding it. I told that when I tried to engage her about the genesis of the idea for the name, all I got were snores in response. Debbie just sat for a moment after I finished and then got a chill that she shook off.

"Wow," she said.

"Just a little freaky, right," says Loretta?

"The subconscious is a complicated place," I said.

"I think that it was an angel that came to you Loretta," says Debbie.

I listen to them muse back and forth and allow my mind to drift away in thought as we enjoy a lovely luncheon. I step out right after to clean up the dishes and give them some private time to chat. As I walk down past the nursing station, there is a bustle of activity that is unusual for this time of the day especially for a Sunday. As I approach, I discern that the commotion is over a scarcity of temperature/blood pressure machines. Walking by the minor conflagration, I notice a familiar face at the center of everything. It's my shift change parking space nemesis. I smile, and she doesn't quite know what to make of me at that moment, so her only reply is to shoot me a puzzled look before she returns to the fray.

While standing in the lobby checking voicemail messages, I see my dad's car drive past the entrance. I figure he's making one circuit of the area before heading for the paid parking lot. Anticipating that he wouldn't find parking on the street at this time of the day on a Sunday, I walk over to that side of the building to meet them as they come in. My wait pays off because after about five minutes, I see them making their way down the street. As expected, my mom sees me first and waves, pointing me out to dad. After focusing, he gives me a wave, and I see his broad smile.

They've probably visited some shut-in church member from their congregation, which is their regular Sunday habit. They still hold hands after all these years, and as they get within ten feet or so, my dad says, "How is the lady, sir?"

"She's well and likely just finishing up a visit with her friend from church," I tell them.

We walk in through the front entrance of the hospital and head for the coffee shop. My dad wants to pick up some flowers to go with the greeting card he has brought.

"I could use some coffee," says my dad.

"I'll have a cup as well. The coffee upstairs is not so good, and I know that Ma'Dear will not turn down a cup of tea."

This brings a smile to the face of Ma'Dear, and she says, "That's what happens when they know your business."

We all laugh as the attendant, who has come to know me quite well, prepares the order.

As we walk down the hall past the NICU, I glance through the vertical window on the left side of the door and see blue clad people milling about in there. It feels now as if *something* should have occurred to me in that moment, some light bulb moment, but nothing did.

"So how is she really?" asks Pop.

"She is as good as one could expect under the circumstances. She is the very essence of a trooper, but it is not easy. I see daily what she endures, and I can tell you that it is not easy. The only solace that I can provide is to be there and hold her hand."

As the elevator door opens, Debbie steps out and says, "Loretta said that there'd be more visitors, so I thought I'd leave to make room. Hi, Mom and Dad. How are you?"

"Ma'Dear, Pop, you remember Debbie," I chime in knowing that they probably would not remember the name.

"Yes, of course. Hello, my dear, how are you?" says Pop rather gushingly.

"I'm doing fine, thanks. I just came to visit a bit with Loretta and Von," replies Debbie.

"And it was quite a lovely visit, I must say," I add.

"How are your girls, Debbie?" asks Ma'Dear.

"They're fine, thank you for asking," says Debbie poorly masking her surprise that Ma'Dear remembered the girls.

One thing about Ma'Dear, she has a special place for children.

"I'll let you folks get up there and see Loretta. It was so good to see you both. You're looking very well. Von, keep me posted, you hear," admonishes Debbie as she turns and walks away.

"I'll do that, ma'am, and thanks for lunch," I reply as we all wave goodbye.

"She brought lunch?" asks Ma'Dear,

"Yes, she surely did," I reply. "She served us on real dinner plates from her home. It was quite a touching gesture, and Loretta was very moved by it."

The elevator door opens, and as we step out, despite the relative calm, I notice that there is a lone PCT at the station. You guessed it, the shift change nemesis. Without looking at her, I reach for my phone and speed dial Loretta's patient advocate. Before we reach the room, and with no one else being the wiser, I have related my concerns, and had her moved to another part of the ward. I'll tell Loretta later.

I hustle ahead of the folks in order to precede them through the curtains. "Hello, ma'am, I have brought visitors bearing gifts," I herald.

Ma'Dear and Pop are beaming as they come through the door, and move to the bedside for hugs and kisses as I immediately retreat from the room in search of a vase. Returning with the vase, I pause at the door and look at the picture before me. Ma'Dear sitting there at the bedside holding Loretta's hand, with Pop standing behind her. It's been twenty-seven days of this for her, and though we're in this for the long haul, I can't help but wonder, how much? Just at that moment, my phone rings.

"Hello?"

"Vonstone, its Sandra Velella. We're on for 10:30 a.m."

"Thank you, Sandra," I'll tell Loretta right away.

"Once I remove the cerclage, you'll be moving you down to a room on the surgical floor, so be prepared, okay?"

"Thank you again, Sandra, we'll be ready."

Loretta, having heard my phone ring and doubtless heard some of the conversation, smiles expectantly as I reenter the room.

"We're on for ten-thirty tomorrow morning," I report to the room triumphantly.

"Thank God," says Ma'Dear, as Loretta sighs relief. The beginning of the end of the month-long discomfort is now in sight, but for all the relief I feel for Loretta, this is but a brief respite. The removal of the cerclage, the last major obstacle to spontaneous delivery, portends great uncertainty ahead.

CHAPTER 7

PERESTROIKA

Monday morning began curiously enough. I worked late into the night in the nursery and went to bed dog-tired at about 1:30 a.m. But unable to sleep a moment longer, I rose at five, showered, dressed, and made a quickie omelet of mushrooms, onions, and cheese, washing it down with a cup of strong black tea, before heading out for the hospital, way too early for any hope of shift change parking. Having gotten out this early, the Monday morning traffic is quite light. I get to the hospital in about ten minutes moving on clear roads bordered by putrid grey snow banks. The hospital emergency entrance is unusually quiet. There are several ambulances idling on the street around the entrance with one in the bay. Having arrived too early for the shift change, I decided not to mess around trying to secure street parking and instead opt to head directly for the parking garage. After making my way to the rooftop, I find the only spot in the entire garage. I encounter a familiar face as the elevator stops on the second floor. It's the PCT with the bad attitude. I do not look at her as she steps onto the elevator and makes her way to the back, but I feel her eyes glaring at the back of my head.

Loretta is asleep when I arrive, so I make my way in and sit quietly in the corner. I find myself wondering if she had a good night, given the expectation of what the morning held. A good night's rest is always in the plan, but she sometimes responds differently to the various nightly rhythms of the ward.

"What are you thinking about?" she says surprising me.

"Hey, sleeping beauty," I reply.

"How long have you been here watching me sleep?"

"I don't know, but I had to push your chin up a couple of times and wipe away drool," I said, managing to contain laughter.

"I was not drooling," she says feigning incredulity.

"I'm kidding, you weren't drooling, but the snoring was audible from down the hall."

"If you are going to harass me, you might have to go back home, sir," says Loretta now fully awake. I smile and put my head back suddenly now a bit dozy now that I'm here.

"You didn't sleep well, I can tell," she says.

"Up at five, no point in trying to go back, so I showered, ate, and came over," I reply. "But oddly, I'm feeling just a bit dozy right now."

"So you should lay back and take a nap because you seem to sleep better here anyway," says Loretta.

"I know, must be the company," I say as I doze off.

I awaken from a really good nap to the Monday morning shift going about their routine in the room. Loretta is sleepily having her temperature and BP taken for the ten thousandth time. "Hey, it's about two hours till go time," I tell her.

"They won't be feeding me, so I'm going back to sleep," says Loretta drawing the covers up to her neck. I respond by closing my eyes, welcoming more sleep. The shift nurse comes in at about nine-forty-five to report that transportation will be coming to get Loretta. She reminds us that we will not be returning to this floor, but instead will be going to labor and delivery post-surgery. I make a mental note of what *I* will need to do to facilitate the move, but there's not much as the maintenance takes everything down on a cart.

"Are you ready?" I ask her.

"I am so ready to have this done with," she replies.

"I'll be right back," I say.

I'm slipping next door to the hospitality room for a cup of coffee, but I avoid any reference to food, as Loretta is likely quite hun-

gry. I spot a kindred spirit in the doorway of a room down the hall
and move toward him.

"Good morning," I say.

"Morning," he replies in a thick Russian accent.

"What are you in for?" I ask jokingly.

"Tvins," he replies holding up two fingers. We both laugh.

"What about you?" he asks.

"The duration," I reply.

Seeing the puzzled look on his face, I add, "I'll be here until she
delivers. One more week, one more month, only God knows. My
name is Vonstone," I say extending my hand.

"Yevgeny," he says meeting my handshake.

I'm about to add some details when I spot transportation coming down from the other end of the hallway.

"Hey, Yevgeny, I've got to go meet these transportation guys,
we'll talk soon, okay?" I said as I headed back toward the room.

"Dasvidaniya Vonstone," I hear behind me.

"Till next time, Yevgeny," I reply as I zero in on the doorway,
getting inside before the transportation team.

"Ready to rock and roll?" I say cheerily as the nurse and Loretta
look curiously in my direction.

They realize that I hadn't lost it when the team followed me into
the room. After verifying the identity of the patient, they transfer
her to the transit bed and we're off. Heading to the internal patient
elevators, we pass by Yevgeny, who waves at us and says, "Udachi,"
which means good luck in Russian.

"Spasibo, Yevgeny," I reply, which means thank you in Russian.
Growing up in Brooklyn gave me access to many languages, so I
learned the basic greetings and responses in a few of them. Yevgeny
looked impressed anyway, smiling broadly.

I look around hoping to see Rachel, the Mennonite nurse
that I met when Loretta had the cerclage put in, to no avail. The
pre-op is pretty busy, and I see a few familiar faces. Having been here
for almost one month, people become readily recognizable to one
another. Loretta is in some discomfort as they begin to connect her to
an IV, through which they will eventually administer the sleep agent.

"They've already given you the oral to relax you, right, I ask?

"Wuzzy, wuzzy," she replies.

Wuzzy, wuzzy is Loretta's description of the medication and the feeling that it induces. I cannot stand the feeling that these drugs bring about; that floating, out of body experience, but Loretta loves it. Her eyes are visibly glassy now, and the words are slurring.

"When you wake up, you'll be going to a new room, remember?" I say trying to gauge her coherence.

She is silent for a bit, and then tells me, "The pine tarts weren't very good this morning, the crust tasted like curry."

Okay, I think to myself, *she's almost out.* The anesthesiologist drops by to "introduce" himself, and Loretta perks up a bit, no more curried pine tart crust commentary. I sit by the bedside and silently hold her hand until they come in to take her into the OR.

I use the time that Loretta is in the OR to visit the room and see to the move. I had her personals with me in my trusty shoulder bag, so all that remained was her hospital gear, and her fridge, if they permitted us to have it in the new space. When I arrived on the floor and began to make my way to the room, I heard a familiar voice say, "You're late again, boss, the work is already done."

It was Andrew, the gentleman that so kindly furnished us with the refrigerator.

"How are you, Andrew? It's good to see you, man," I said.

"The move has already been accomplished, sir, and the room is in readiness."

"Terrific, Andrew, I'm going down to get some coffee and a muffin with the time you've bought me, would you care to join me?"

"I was actually just on my way down for my break, thank you, I will join you," said Andrew.

The two of us pass a very pleasant fifteen minutes over coffee, where Andrew shares his dream of returning to Trinidad and opening a shoe repair shop, but says that his wife will have none of it. I guess this dream will necessarily be deferred. Andrew heads over to the ambulance bay, promising to come and check on us, while I head back inside to await the completion of the procedure. On my way in, I decide to stop in to check out the new digs. It's pretty quiet at the moment, and all the staff appears to be at the nurses' station milling and discussing. I saunter over and inquire as to where 'my patient' will reside, and they point the way. The room is significantly smaller than the prior two accommodations, but it is by no means uncomfortable. Having reconnoitered the new accommodations, I resume my original heading, the OR in which Loretta was being de-cerclaged.

As I approach the waiting area, I hear a familiar voice.

"Can I get you anything, Mr. Wolfe?"

It's Rachel.

"Your timing is perfect. They've just taken her into recovery," Rachel reports.

"Well hello, Rachel, how wonderful it is to see you. I looked for you earlier when we came down," I tell her.

"I was otherwise engaged. May I take you back?" she offers.

"Why yes, of course, Rachel, by all means, let's go," I eagerly accept. Dr. Velella is coming into the recovery room at the same moment. "Mr. Wolfe, I was just about to come out looking for you."

"Hello, Dr. Velella; how did everything go?"

"The procedure went well, all things considered," she says as I hold my breath. "There was a great deal of inflammation as the urethra swelled through the stitches. It was necessary for me to do some cutting to access the stitches, so she's going to be a bit sore for a few days, but that is the extent of the *surgical* difficulty. As we discussed previously, we'll be doing the steroid injection this afternoon and we'll continue the magnesium sulfate IV to try and slow him down. Do you have any questions for me?" asks the doctor.

"Will she be able to eat lunch," I ask.

"Yes, and you'll give her lots and lots of fluids. You have my direct number, so if anything comes up, let me hear from you first. You'll be here, right?" she asks.

"Yes, ma'am, I am here for the duration," I reply definitely.

"Good because nothing is more important than being present here with her," advises the doctor.

"Believe me, doctor, if I don't know anything else, I know that," I reply.

"I'm glad of that, Mr. Wolfe," she says. "Good luck, and call me if you need me," says the doctor as she breezes out of the recovery room.

I turn to find Loretta's beautiful hazel eyes looking at me over the oxygen mask. I stand and lean over the bed, kissing her forehead, and giving her hand a squeeze. She squeezes back, but retains control of my hand, forcing me to pull the chair over with my extended foot. I sit there with her clutching my hand for about ten minutes until she says, "Will you be needing that back?"

"Eventually," I say smiling. "I thought you were asleep, ma'am."

"No, just resting quietly," she replies.

Just then, the recovery room nurse comes in and takes Loretta's vitals. We're releasing you to labor and delivery Loretta. She gives the nurse a confused look, and I chime in, "Yes, thank you, nurse, we're aware?"

I make certain that when Loretta awakens in her new room, I am at the bedside. I did not wish her to awaken in a strange new room in an anesthesia fog.

"You again. Are you still stalking me?" she says.

"What gave it away? I thought that I was observing my very best stalking techniques," I reply. "Are you hungry, I've put aside some pine tarts with curry flavored crust for you?"

"Okay, where is that coming from?" she asks with a smile.

"Just picking up on our conversation just before you went under, my dear," I explain.

"I am half starving though; what do they have," asks Loretta?

"I put aside your lunch of herb-baked chicken breast and mixed vegetables, chicken broth, and Jell-o. Otherwise, I can rustle up a sandwich and a cup of tea. The choice is yours, ma'am," I reply.

"I think I'll try the chicken," says Loretta after a few deliberative seconds.

"I'll warm it up and bring a cup of tea with it," I tell her.

Returning from a chat with the charge nurse down at the nurse's station, regarding the scheduled time of the steroid injections as well as the type of monitoring that will be done, I find Loretta fast asleep. I return to the station to ask what pain meds had been prescribed by the doctor for the soreness that was inevitable after the procedure. Having received competent assurance from the nurse that there was an order placed, I returned to Loretta's side. I notice a collection of sandwiches on my way back, so I grab a tuna and a milk.

I clear the lunch tray from the room and return, where I sit and eat my sandwich in absolute silence. About an hour later, the nurse comes in to administer pain meds (squeaky wheel baby). The nurse says that she'll sleep for a while and that's good. As she said that, Loretta woke up and said, "What's up?"

"Pain meds," I said.

"Wuzzy Wuzzy," she asks.

"Not likely," I said looking at the nurse for confirmation.

All I got was a puzzled look.

"What the hell is wuzzy wuzzy?" she asked breaking into laughter.

"Oxy, or its generic equivalent," I reply.

"Not today, missy. All I have for you today is Tylenol," replies the nurse to Loretta who feigns disappointment (I think).

Loretta takes the pain med while I talk to the nurse, who explains what the monitoring regime will look like. I turn to Loretta asking, "Did you get all that, ma'am?"

As I look over at her, I realize that she's out again.

Since initial discussion surrounding the removal of the cerclage, my thoughts uncontrollably wander to the eventuality of a premature birth. I have not had the courage to yet share these thoughts with Loretta, but that moment is coming. I leave labor and delivery and wander over to the NICU where I encounter a couple walking out. I smile and nod at them, but they do not smile back. I just get a polite but distant nod from the husband. I walk over to the gift shop to purchase a big bottle of water. I walk back to the elevator by way of the NICU, and outside the main door, I see the couple that had exited as I walked past the first time. They look up as I approach, and I say, "Good afternoon."

"Afternoon," says the husband as his wife nods. "Do you have a baby in there?" asks the husband.

"No, actually my wife is around the corner in labor and delivery. She's just had a cerclage removed," I tell them.

"I'm Brian, by the way; my wife also had a cerclage. Bought us some valuable time," says Brian.

I look over at the woman who immediately says, "Oh no, that's not me, that would be my sister, Ava," she corrects. "I'm Natalie."

"I'm so sorry, I just assumed, seeing the two of you together that you were …"

"No problem," says Natalie, "it was a natural assumption. When we came out earlier, I was a bit upset because they were suctioning Rachel, and it can be somewhat unpleasant."

"It shouldn't be much longer now. I think that we can see the end of the tunnel," says Brian.

Just then the door is flung wide open, a woman steps out and moves in our direction. This must be Ava because both Brian and Natalie say a quick goodbye and move to meet her.

Making my way back to labor a delivery I notice some cookies there and stop to make two cups of tea. This was most fortuitous, because Loretta is awake and feeling peckish.

"What've you got there?" she says.

"I've brought you a little afternoon snack," I reply. "Cookies. How's your pain?"

"I'm really sore," she says grimacing.

"You have every right to be. The doctor says that they had to do some cutting to get to the cerclage."

"That's why I'm so sore. I may need something a bit stronger," says Loretta, suddenly acutely aware of the pain.

"It's been prescribed, just in case you needed it. I'll tell your nurse."

The unexpected treat is definitely one to savor, and Loretta appears to relish the afternoon delight of tea and cookies. Being in this particularly antiseptic hospital setting causes one to appreciate the little things that perhaps might be enjoyed in the more genial atmosphere of home.

"I was at the NICU just a while ago, well, outside anyway," I report to Loretta.

"Oh," she said probingly?

"I walked by, just to get a sense of the place, I guess."

"What'd you come away with?"

"I don't quite know. I spoke to some folks with a baby inside and ..."

"Really?" she exclaims. "How premature is their baby? What did they have to say about the care? How often are they able to visit?"

"We didn't get to any of that. I spoke briefly with the dad and sister-in-law—whom I initially believed to be the wife. By the time we got that cleared up, the wife came out of the NICU, and the team rallied to her. They did mention that the suctioning of the baby, whatever that is, was a bit unpleasant though."

"I know, words and actions can affect reality, but I just wanted to get a sense of the place," I tell her.

"In your place, I would have done the same. I understand why you feel the need," she said.

I am glad that Loretta feels that way because I am going to be frequenting the NICU hallway in the coming days.

"Knock, knock, imaging," says a voice from the hall.

It was the ultrasound operator. This imaging was going to be routine in the coming days in order to monitor any changes in the position of the baby and dilation of the urethra.

"Come on in," says Loretta in a cheerful voice.

The operator enters quietly, accompanied by the whirs and clicks of the motor in the unit. She talks her way through the procedure as we crane expectantly at the monitor to get a glimpse of our boy. This is our way to visually connect with him.

"Hey, buddy. How are you today?" I say to him as mommy smiles.

The technician wraps up her work and bids us a see you later before disappearing behind the curtain. I get up and run some warm water in a basin. Using one of our soft washcloths from home, I gently wipe away the stickiness of the KY Jelly.

"That feels good," says Loretta, and I keep it up until the water begins to cool down.

I get a fresh basin of warm water and tidy her up for the evening, paying particular attention to her feet. I attire her in a fresh double gown ensemble and pronounce her *ready for the world.*

"I feel good; a bit sore, but overall I feel good. Thank you," she says.

"It is, my dear, the smallest of things that I can do. You have the infinitely harder part, and if I can do some small thing to give you comfort, it is but a small thing," I assure her. "I think that a haircut is in order. What do you think, ma'am?"

"Nah, well maybe, we'll see," she says indecisively.

"Hey, for twenty-four weeks and five days, the little boy has stayed put inside you," I said.

"And each and every day, we pray, for just another day," says Loretta.

We hold each other's hand as we share the thought expressed by Loretta. *Just one more day, each day, just one more day.*

Dinner arrives, and I set up the tray in front of her. Meatloaf, or some facsimile thereof, and broccoli. "Would you like a tray sir," asks the food service lady?

"Why yes, thank you, miss, I believe I will."

Looking over at Loretta, I see the absolute shock upon her face. When the young lady leaves to retrieve a tray for me, Loretta can contain herself no longer.

"You're going to actually eat something other than a sandwich?" she asks.

"Yes, I'm feeling adventurous this evening, ma'am."

"My, my, my, will wonders never cease," she teases?

"Come on now, it's not that much of a surprise, is it?"

"There are certainly greater things to ponder in the grand scheme of things."

"That's true, but you've never graced the kitchens of this hospital by eating their food," says Loretta.

"Hey, they make the sandwiches, don't they?" I shot back.

The young lady reenters the room with my tray, and I rise to take it from her. "I could use a cold beverage. I thing I'll get a couple of those juices," I say.

I zip across the hall and grab a couple of juices. Walking back. I notice a familiar figure standing down the hall—it's Yevgeny standing in the doorway waving to me. I wave back, smile, and go back to my dinner date. I tell Loretta about how I met Yevgeny upstairs on the maternity floor, and that they are, once again, her neighbors in labor and delivery.

"How's your dinner?" asks Loretta. "Is it all that you expected?"

"It actually isn't too bad, about what I'd expect, I think, how about yours?"

"It's okay, but I think I'm ready for some home food," says the patient.

"You know, as I ate I was thinking the same thought. What is your palate telling you?"

With absolutely no hesitation, Loretta gave me the menu for tomorrow's meal.

"I'd like brown stewed turkey wings, rice and peas, with plantains, and steamed cabbage and carrots."

"Wow, you've really thought this through, haven't you?" I reply laughing.

"Lying here half-way upside down, day after day, I have a lot of time to do just that. Reading makes me nauseous, and while watching this daytime programming, I can feel my brain devolving," she explains. I make a mental note to bring a book and begin reading to her while I am here, and curse myself for not having anticipated this need.

"Point taken. Your menu has been dually noted and will be served to you for tomorrows dinner," I assure her.

Rising from my chair, I tell Loretta that I need to run a couple of errands, and that I'd be back by shift change. Clearing the lunch trays to the sink-top, I kiss her and skitter out of the room. As I pass the room where I had seen Yevgeny, I knock and call out.

"Dobriy vyecher Yevgeny," I call out.

A laugh booms from inside the room.

"Preevyet Vonstone, please come in and meet my beloved," invites Yevgeny.

"Preevyet," as I nod once to each of them.

Yevgeny's wife is unable to contain her shock when I part the curtains and enter the room.

"Vonstone, meet my beloved, Olga. Olga, my new friend, Vonstone," says Yevgeny making the introduction.

"Nice to meet you," says Olga.

Yev has told me *some* things about you. He has a marvelous economy for ignoring irrelevant details." We all share a knowing laugh.

"The pleasure is all mine, Olga," I reply. "So I imagine you're close," I say looking at Olga.

"Sure feels like it," says Olga rubbing her enormous belly.

"I do hate to cut this short, but I have a couple of errands to run and be back before the shift change," I explain.

"You'll be staying here with your wife?" asks Olga.

"I feel like I live here," I reply. "Olga, it was nice meeting you," I say as I wave to Yevgeny and head for the door.

I pull the curtain behind me, exit the room, and start down the hall. Just then, I hear a voice behind me as I am about to exit the unit.

"Vonstone, just one minute," says Yevgeny. "I wonder if you and I could kill a single bird with two stones."

I laugh out loud. "That would be a most inefficient use of stones, my friend. I think that the euphemism that you seek is killing two birds with one stone," I tell him. "What do you have in mind, Yevgeny?"

"The same as you, a few errands, and we can have good conversation. I'll drive, okay?"

"Sounds great Yevgeny, but if it's all the same to you, I will drive, only because I have to get my car out of the parking garage onto the street," I explain.

"Okay, I will kiss Olga, and we'll go," says Yevgeny.

We talk about how much he and Olga love New York, and how they're saving to buy a home in Brighton Beach, Brooklyn. I tell Yev that I've been all over this state, and I love Brooklyn the most. I tell him, "If you don't see me around Brooklyn, I've left the state, because I won't live anywhere else in New York State."

I drop Yev off at home off of New Utrecht Ave., and we agree on a ninety-minute turnaround. This will give him time to pick up some goodies for Olga and for me to hit the supermarket for a few grocery items for tomorrow's promised dinner.

I swing by Shoprite and gather the needed items and head home. I scan the mail quickly and separate the bills into the action pile on the rack above the kitchen island. I begin cleaning and seasoning the meat, being very mindful of the time. After doing all the prep work for the meal, I have time for a quick shower before heading out to pick up Yev, leaving us thirty minutes to get back for the shift change.

Headed through the den, I grab a volume of Tolstoy, portions of which I fully intend to read to Loretta. As I walk to the car in the driveway, our neighbor, Jean, appears on the porch of her home.

"Hello, Vonstone, how is Loretta?" she asks.

"She's doing well, all things considered, Jean," I reply. "Loretta is a trooper, a real trooper."

"Give her my love and these goodies. You're both in my prayers."

"I will, Jean. Thanks for the goodies. We appreciate it very much, and have a pleasant evening."

She remains on the porch waving as I back out of the driveway, and I wave to her as I pull away. Good old Jean, such a gem. I avoid Church Ave., as the one lane, heavily trafficked artery is a nightmare at this time. I squirrel through a myriad of side streets, emerging onto McDonald Ave. and slicing through Borough Park to New Utrecht Ave, and 53rd Street, where Yevgeny is waiting on the steps in front of his apartment building.

"Wow, you have good timing, Vonstone," says Yev. "I am accustomed to being on time, being a limousine driver, and it ticks me off when people don't respect my time, so thank you sir."

"You're very welcome, Yev," I reply. We have less than a ten-minute drive to the hospital and more than twenty five minutes to the shift change. That turns out to be a good thing because we run into about ten minutes of traffic trying to work our way up to the hospital. We arrive still with fifteen minutes to spare, and as the parking gods reward the prepared, we are blessed with a parking spot as we turn onto Ft. Hamilton Pkwy.

"*Chert vozʹmi, da,*" exults Yev!

"Okay, you got me, Yev. What does that mean?" I ask.

"Loosely translated, it means, hell yeah," Yev explains.

"Okay then, *chert vozʹmi, da,*" I join in!

As we walk up 49th Street toward 10th Avenue. Yev says, "This was really fun, Vonstone. We must seek opportunities to spent time together, you and me. I think we are of a kind, Vonstone."

"I agree, Yev. We must get together when things settle down. But for now, we're here, right?

"Right," says Yev as we walk through the main entrance of the hospital.

"Can I help you gentlemen?" says a guard whose face is unfamiliar to me?

Yev and I look at each other, then back toward the guard, and I say, "No, we're good. Thank you though."

The whole time, we never stop walking, so by the time we issue our reply, we're already past him. He beacons us back and we tacitly agree to ignore him. As we're walking away, never turning around mind you, we hear the voice of another guard telling him to calm down.

"What the hell was that," I say to Yev?

"Asshole, he's probably new and doesn't know his way yet," says Yev.

"You're probably right. I don't remember ever seeing him before," I reply.

We enter the unit, and as we approach Olga's room, Yev says, "*spokoynoy nochi*, Vonstone."

"Is that good night?"

"Yes."

"Then *spokoynoy nochi*, Yevgeny to you and Olga."

CHAPTER 8

NNP HAMMERHAND

The morning monitoring regime is the most important regular happening in our lives. We seem to live from ultrasound to ultrasound; hoping and praying that nothing (much) changes from day to day. The war of attrition, however, is being waged by the precious little life inside Loretta. His desire to come out is strong, as evidenced by the latest ultrasound.

"We are engaged in a delaying action here, as we have previously discussed. We can only hope to delay, for as long as possible, the inevitability of a premature birth," says Dr. Velella. "This is what we must prepare for."

We hear these words every few days, and we are not, by any means, unimpressed by all that they imply, but hope is a funny thing. Through all of Dr. Velella's exhortations and counsel, we always have faith that the best possible outcome will be ours. We never entertain any outcome that is not absolutely in our favor. Loretta, in particular, believes in the formative ability of words to mold reality.

"We are all on the same page, doctor. We will do all that is asked and anything else," says Loretta.

"Good, I like the energy I'm getting here," says Sandra Velella. "We'll do this again in a couple of days guys. Keep up the energy and stay in the positive."

"Thanks, doctor," we say almost in unison.

"How're you feeling after all that activity?" I ask.

"Just a bit fatigued, and you?" asks Loretta jokingly.

"I'm just happy to have seen my son again. What do you mean by fatigued? Is there any pain, discomfort, or pressure?" I ask.

"All very good questions, but I think I'm just tired."

"You know me, I've got to ask," I tell her smiling.

Just then my phone rings, and it's Will. "Sup, brother?"

"Big Willy Style!! What's up, my brother?"

"I'm good, man. How's the missus doing?"

"She's rightfully tired, man. She's had a busy morning so far, and didn't sleep very well last night," I share.

"Say hello for me please," says Loretta almost sleepily.

"Will, Loretta says hi," I tell him.

"Give the lady my regards in return. Listen, she sounds really tired, so I'm gonna let you go," says Will.

"Thanks for reaching out, man. I'll keep you posted, okay." I reply?

"Peace," he says in his signature sign-off.

I make a mental note to send an update to my previously created distribution list. Breakfast arrives, and Loretta makes a point of reminding me about dinner.

"I did not forget, ma'am. The meat is marinating as we speak and the peas are soaking."

"I can just taste it," she drools.

"I'm on the case, ma'am. I'm going to put in a few hours in the nursery today when I get back from the gym, so I'll cook whilst I work," I tell her.

I get the basin of warm water and begin the ritual of tidying her up. The PCT comes in and offers to take care of her, and Loretta gives me the nod.

"Why don't you get started with your day, sir?" she says.

"Quicker I leave, quicker I'm back, right?"

"Exactly," she says. "Now you're getting it," she says as we all have a laugh.

"I'll take good care of her, don't worry," says the PCT.

I kiss Loretta and make my way toward the elevator. I think about Yevgeny and Olga as I pass her room, but don't wish to disturb, so I keep on toward the elevator. Ft. Hamilton Pkwy is busy as expected for a weekday morning, but I'm moving relatively against traffic. I'm able to get home pretty quickly where I make a quick smoothie, set up my work in the nursery for later and pack my gym bag.

I call Will's number on my way out the door, and he tells me he's already on the road.

Will is about six feet two inches, and about 260 pounds of solid muscle. I cannot lift with Will if he's lifting seriously, but we have agreed that we are getting old and must adopt a challenging but sane routine. This is the framework within which we operate.

When I walk out onto the gym floor, I see my former workout partner, Hugh. gearing up for a morning workout. Hugh, at this time, is a competitive power lifter, and because he is here in the morning means that there is a competition brewing. He does twice a day workouts when preparing for a competition.

"Ross, good morning," I salute him.

"Vonstone, how is your wife," he asks?

"She's good, man. I've got to get it done and get back," I tell him.

Just then, Will walks up.

"Ross, Wolfe," says Will.

"Smith," says Hugh.

"Good, you're here," I reply.

Sensing a chat-fest coming on, Ross says, "Okay, gentlemen, let's get to work."

"Good to see you, Ross, have a good workout," I say, and Will waves as we walk away.

Will and I head down to the cardio end of the enormous gym floor as Ross goes into his blackout zone.

"It's cold as shit out there this morning," says Smiddy.

"I know, I can't wait to get off the street. I've got a lot of work to do today," I tell him.

"Got time for a little breakfast once we finish up the workout," asks Will?

"I'd better not man because I've got to work in the nursery for a few hours, and I promised the missus a home cooked meal today."

"What's on the menu?" asks Will.

"Stewed turkey wings, rice and peas, fried plantains, with carrots and cabbage," I reply.

"Why don't you drop over later for a taste?" I tell Will.

"You know me, bruh, I never turn down good food. I'll be there. What time is good?"

"It'll be done by about two, I think."

"Cool, I'll call before I swing by."

One thing about my friend, Will, no matter what the arrangement was, he'd never just drops by; he always calls first. We might have just spoken an hour before, he'd always call. We finish up the workout about ten, and I head out to the showers as Will heads for the steam room. It is quite cold this morning in Brooklyn. Usually, there are people on the street talking, smoking, or standing around outside on the phone, but today is different. The sidewalks are bare of everything but evaporating piles of stale snow. I weave across Brooklyn, mostly doing the side street thing, and arrive back in our neighborhood by about ten-twenty. As I open the door, I hear the house phone chirping.

"Hello?"

"Good morning, this is your mother speaking."

"Hello, Ma'Dear. How are you today?"

"I'm fine, son, how is my daughter?"

"Oh, she's doing pretty well, all things considered," I report. "I think we're getting close, Ma'Dear."

"Oh, I hope she can hold on, but I'm praying, whatever happens, know your mom is holding you three in prayer."

"Thank you, Ma'Dearest, that means a lot."

We chat for about thirty minutes until I hear the alarm chirp, meaning that my dad had just come in from wherever. She tells him that I'm on the phone, and I hear him say, "Hi son," without taking the phone.

"Tell Pop that I'm making stewed turkey wings with rice and peas today."

As she gives the report, I hear my dad in the background say expectantly, "Is my son offering us dinner?"

"Why don't you all stop by this afternoon about two, and you can view the progress on your grandson's nursery?"

"We'll be there," the reply comes back briskly!

I place a call to Loretta to see how her morning is coming along and her cell rings out. I know that she has her cell on vibrate and not wanting to wake her with the room phone, I call the nursing station for a report. She's resting quite comfortably when last her vitals were taken. Reassured that everything is right with Loretta, I plow into the tasks of the day and get to choppin', slicin', steamin', stewin', fryin', sheet rockin', and tapin'.

By one o'clock, the meal is prepared, and I decide to leave the portioning of the food to the one who does it best, Ma'Dear. I finish up taping all the corners in the nursery. All that remains is to sand it absolutely smooth and paint. I have some ideas on what I want it to look like. As with everything construction related, there's a Home Depot book for that (several actually). I'll run my ideas by Loretta later, as I have the books packed in my bag.

It's about five of two, and I've just finished shaving and am pulling on my pants when I hear my doorbell ring. I continue to dress, and when I don't hear any activity, I realize that Will must be on the porch with my parents, or they'd have let themselves in with their key. Rushing down to the door, I hear thunderous laughter on the other side. Yup, they're all out there.

"Welcome, lunch mates, please come in," I bid them.

Everyone comes in, removes their shoes, and head upstairs. The kitchen is the heart of our house. When I did the redesign, I created a very spacious kitchen, with a huge, high island with barstools, lighted mullion door cabinets and countertops lighting. It is quite a comfortable space, and I like to spend time here with guests.

"Man, Wolfe, that smells good," says Will.

"I do hope that it doesn't stop with the smell," says my dad.

Ma'Dear shoots him a look, and I say, "Ma'Dear, its okay, Will's family," smiling.

"Who's hungry, now, and who's takin' it with 'em?" I ask.

"I'd planned to takeout, but since it's a luncheon, I guess I'll eat in," says my dad.

"I cooked plenty, and I only need dinner for Loretta, and I so you all can do both, eat in, and take away. How's that?" I ask.

"Damn decent of you old man," says Will. "You know that …"

"I know, you never turn down good food," I interrupt.

We all share a good laugh.

"Ma'Dear?" She instinctively slides off of her stool and heads for the stove.

"Can I offer a drink to two thirsty gentlemen?"

"Need you ask?" says my dad.

I bring out the scotch and a couple of cans of ginger ale.

"Ma'Dear, tea?"

She nods once, and I turn on the kettle on the countertop.

We enjoy a delightful lunch, and I show everyone the nursery project. Every time Will sits in my kitchen, he always marvels at the fact that I did the entire redesign on my own. He says that if he had not been there during the course of the project, he wouldn't believe it. Dad gushes and says, "My son has gone where I dare not trod," holding up his glass.

"Well, folks, as nice as it is to be here, I'll have to be leaving you now. I got to relieve the missus with junior," says Will.

"Will, it's always so nice to see you," says Ma'Dear hugging his big neck as he bends over.

"Good, sir, it was nice to see you again," says dad shaking his hand. I walk him to the door, and he says, "Thanks for lunch Vonstone."

"Anytime, Will," I say patting his enormous shoulder. "I'll call you on the weekend."

"Peace." I head back to the kitchen where my dad is finishing up his scotch and ginger, and Ma'Dear is washing the pots.

"Are we all packed up?" I ask.

"Mom has taken care of everything," says Pop.

Everything is packed up, and I put our dinner into a thermal bag.

"This was a meal fit for a king," says Pop leaning back in his chair downing the last of his scotch.

Ma'Dear smiles broadly, nodding agreement. We all go out together and share a hug on the porch before parting.

The trip back to the hospital was uncharacteristically quick for this time of the day. I knew going in that I'd have to head for the parking deck, but the parking gods smiled warmly upon me once again as a green Mazda pulled off just as I indicated the left turn. I turned into the spot directly in front of the drive into the lot. Another driver cruised past and eyed me enviously, with a smile.

Loretta is awake when I arrive, and smiles as I walk in with the thermal bag of goodies. "Wooo," she says. "Is that what I think it is?"

"Yup," I replied. "And I have it on well-founded authority that this food is fit for a king."

"Who says that ...?"

"I fed Ma'Dear, Pop, and Will for lunch," I tell her.

"Seriously?" says Loretta laughing. "When did that all that come together?"

I explain that I invited Will after our workout at the gym, and Ma'Dear and Pop after they called later on that morning.

"So I have a meal fit for a king to look forward to then," she asks?

"Well, in your case, a meal fit for a queen."

Laughing she says, "I can't wait, what time is dinner?"

"Anytime that suits you, ma'am. I'm on your schedule," I reply.

"Did you eat with your lunch guests?"

"I tasted a bit of rice with some of the stew gravy, so I'm ready to eat when you are ma'am."

"What time is it now?" she asks.

"About four-thirty," I say. "Did you cancel dinner?"

"Yes, I did, so let's eat, man!"

I rise quickly, wash my hands, and move over to the thermal bag containing our supper. Sharing two plates with all the goodies, I glance over at Loretta, who is smiling broadly.

"Smells good, huh," I say.

She nods yes, smiling at the plate that I'm placing before her. We enjoy our dinner in relative silence, punctuated by the occasional commentary on the dinner itself. As we finish up, Joyce, from food services, sticks her head in to say, "No wonder you didn't want my dinner, Loretta."

We all laugh, and Loretta says that home-cooked food is the best, to which Joyce replies, "I know that's right."

After dinner, I walk down to the gift shop to get a cup of coffee to go with Jean's goodies. There is a woman in front of me that has just purchased a cup of coffee. She's wearing blue Maimonides scrubs and a white smock. "That better not be the last of the coffee ma'am," I say.

"Oh my goodness, I think it might have been," she says. "What are we going to do?"

"You might have to share," I say to her.

The sales clerk, not getting the humor of it all, says, "No, no, I've got another pot right there," he assures us.

We look at him, then each other and laugh out loud.

"Vonstone Wolfe," I say extending my hand.

"Lynn Hammerhand," she says in response. "What are you in for?"

"We've been here for almost a month because we've been experiencing some difficulty keeping the little fella inside. We think that it won't be long now," I reply.

"Just know that there are things that we can do now for preemies, which we couldn't do ten, or even five years ago. Let me say though, that you've got the right attitude, saying we, I mean. That means that you recognize that the two of you are in this together. We can do a lot of things medically here, but people need to have an awareness of the non-medical aspect of this type of care. I gotta go, but we may see each other again, Vonstone."

"Tally ho, Lynn," I reply as she disappears briskly around a corner.

Walking back past the NICU, I glance through the slim traffic window in the door and see lots of activity on the other side near the desk. As I make my way back to labor and delivery, I walk past Olga's room. The door is open, but the curtain is drawn and it is quiet, so I keep going.

"I have your dessert, ma'am," I say as I enter the room. "May I pour you a cup of tea?" I say gesturing to the Thermos in the bag.

She nods, smiling as I pour the tea, and place one of Jean's sesame loafs in front of her. She smiles knowingly and breaks it in half.

CHAPTER 9

BREAKING DAWN

The weekend was intentionally uneventful because Loretta has been in increasing discomfort. She is feeling more and more pressure in her lower abdomen and is constipated beyond human imagining. I hear someone at the door and turn to see a PCT parting the curtain with a blue-gloved hand. Seeing my head raised in the dim light of the room, she says, "Good morning, sorry to disturb you."

"Good morning, no problem, please come on in," I reply.

She parts the curtain with her gloved hand and glides across the tiny room almost silently, the only sound being the swishing sound that her uniform made as she walked. Moving to the bedside, she collects the bedpan and takes it into the bathroom to measure Loretta's urine output. Emanating from the bathroom are sounds of pouring flushing and rinsing, followed by her appearance in the doorway, bedpan in hand. She moves *directly* to Loretta's bedside and reaches for the thermometer to take her temperature.

"Stop! What are you doing?" I exclaim.

"I'm going to take her BP and temp," she replies sounding a bit shocked.

"Will you be changing those gloves first?" I ask, being very deliberate with the words.

Her reply shocks me right down to my socks.

"No, they're clean, see ..." she says holding up both hands with fingers spread, rotating them back to front for maximum viewing of any germs that may be present.

I was stunned beyond words and sat up in my cot my mind formulating a response.

"What does a germ look like?" I ask her.

"Huh?"

"I said, what–does–a–germ–look–like?"

Before she could respond, I ask a follow-up question. "If there was a germ on your glove, would you be able to see it?" She looks perplexed and cornered, but I'm merciless and pounce. "Get out, and don't come back!"

She turns and races from the room, momentarily becoming tangled in the curtain.

Loretta says, "I'm so glad that you were awake and caught all of that."

I was so angry that I felt my face flush. A few moments later, there is a knock at the door and the doctor comes through the curtains.

"Good morning, Loretta," says the doctor.

Loretta was on her side and facing away from him at that moment. Without turning to look at him, she points at me in a manner, which suggested to the doctor that he needed to speak to me.

The doctor turned toward me and opened his mouth to speak, but I cut him off before he'd uttered a single word.

"Look, I don't know what kind of operation you've got going here, doctor, but apparently your PCTs think that it's okay to float in here wearing a pair of gloves and perform all her duties in here and leave with the same gloves. She furthermore thinks that just because a pair of gloves isn't visibly soiled, then they're okay for continued use," I tell him. "Perhaps that's okay with you folks, but I assure you, sir, it is wholly unacceptable to us. I don't want that PCT back in here, period!"

"I understand your concerns, sir, but we're a bit short tonight and ..."

"Doctor, you'd better find us a less hygienically challenged PCT to do this because that one won't be doing anything in this room ever again," I shot back.

"Sir, we need to get these readings recorded and ..."

"Then why are you wasting your breath standing here arguing with me when I have already told you that the 'dirty hands' PCT will not be allowed back in here? I'm not changing my mind on this, so let's get it done."

He walks out shaking his head, and I hear him in a conversation outside the room with, who could only be, madam dirty hands herself.

After he leaves, I hear Loretta say in a quiet voice tinged with pain, "Thank you, honey."

"I got this, don't worry," I assure her.

I rise and take up a position outside the room to intercept any more disturbances to her rest.

About fifteen minutes later, I see the doctor reenter L&D with another doctor in tow. As they approach the room, the other doctor introduces himself and asks if he may enter. We step inside, he grabs a pair of large gloves, and proceeds to examine Loretta. He then wheels over the vitals cart, changes his gloves again, and begins taking her vital signs.

I look over at doctor number one and say, "Are you taking notes?"

He looks verily annoyed, as he did not expect that this was what was going to happen. The doctor wraps up and whispers something to Loretta and pats my shoulder with a smile as he passes me. They both exit into the corridor, as I look over smiling at Loretta. I step into the hall in time to hear the chief attending say that, "Sometimes being a doctor means doing what must be done."

"I do hope you learned something here today, young man," I scold jokingly.

"Goodnight, sir," he says coldly.

He walks past Yevgeny, who had just entered L&D.

"He looked pissed, Vonstone. What did you do to him?" asks Yev.

"His boss just kicked his tail up his ass with the shiniest most diplomatic shoe that I have ever seen," I tell him. "It was indeed a pleasure to watch."

"Hmm," says Yev, not quite understanding.

"Just make sure that when the PCT comes in, that she changes her gloves after emptying the bedpan, okay? I'll tell you all about it later."

"Gotcha, thanks, Vonstone," he replies.

Reentering the room quietly, I sit in the chair because I am confident that I will not be able to find sleep again, being as worked up as I currently am.

"The doctor says that you did the right thing," says Loretta in a sleepy voice.

"He kicked the other one in the ass right outside the room. I heard a little bit of it as I stepped outside. I'll tell you about it later," I tell her.

She just grunts a response, and it becomes plain to me that we were on the cusp of labor. Not quite to the point of measuring contractions, but certainly on the cusp.

I must have dozed off at some point because when my eyes opened, we were in the midst of the shift change. A chunky, pleasant woman entered the room and introduced herself as Loretta's nurse. She asks Loretta, who was awake but not really paying attention because of the pain, to rate her pain using the scale. She bangs in at a consistent seven. The ultrasound reveals jut why the pain is so intense; there is no further doubt that Loretta is in labor.

"Its official," I tell her. "We're in the countdown now, ma'am. I know that we've talked about this time and that we approach it with mixed feelings. On one hand, the pain and difficulty of this pregnancy drawing to a close, but on the other, the short road of the pregnancy leaves us a longer and more difficult road for our son."

She lay on her side with her back turned to me, and I knew that there were tears, partly because of what I had said, but partly because of the helplessness of the situation.

We, and the doctors, had done everything that could be done, and now all our hopes for this little boy rested on prayers that so many others had breathed into the universe on his behalf. I reach up to the bed and place my hand on her side. She reaches over, grasps my hand tightly, and sobs audibly. I move onto the bed and hug her.

"He's coming, because of our prayers, our belief, our desire, our tears, and science. When he is here, it's our prayers, desire, tears, and science that will sustain him," I comfort.

We hug silently.

"I would endure this pain for another six months to give him a better chance," she replies.

"I know you would, honey," I reply.

I cross the room to the sink where I turn hot water faucet, retrieve the basin from the sink vanity, and fill it with warm water. Gathering her toiletries, a fresh gown and towels, I return to the bedside, bring the bed to 180 degrees, gently remove her gown, and begin tidying her up. I spend a long time allowing the warm water to play on her belly.

"That fells absolutely wonderful, but the bed is going to be soaked," says Loretta.

"Speaking of which …"

I press the call button and tell the nursing station that we'll need the linens changed. I proceed to lotion her, again spending a lot of time on the belly. By the time the PCT arrives to change the linens, she's brushing her teeth and in a much better mood, pain notwithstanding.

"Good morning," says Loretta. "What's your name?"

"Good morning, miss, my name is Audrey, and I'm here to change your linens. I see that you've been cleaned up already," she says smiling.

"I'll hop right out of your way," says Loretta as I help her off of the bed.

"Aren't we feeling spry this morning? All hoppy and stuff," I tease her.

"That sponge bath was just what the doctor ordered," she replied as I ease her down into the recliner. From just outside, the door a voice is heard.

"Knock, knock, I didn't order any sponge bath, though I probably should have because it's always a good idea."

"Good morning, Dr. Kelly," says Loretta.

"Good morning Loretta, Mr. Wolfe," says Dr. Kelly. "I understand that you're having a hard time. How's your pain today, Loretta?" says the doctor softly.

"I feel like I'm at about an eight this morning doctor," says Loretta wincing a bit and rocking back and forth.

"Is the pain fluctuating between more intense pain and less intense pain?" asks the doctor.

"Yes, it really hurts for about half a minute and then subsides. Dr. Wolfe here is sure that they are contractions, but no one here has used the 'c' word," says Loretta.

"Well, Dr. Wolfe is right. Just sitting here, it is clear to me that you're experiencing labor contractions," says the real doctor.

Turning to me the doctor asks, "Do you know what to look for and how to measure the contractions?"

"Yes, I do. Contractions vary in intensity, lasting from thirty to forty seconds and become critical when the interval between them is four minutes or less. So, I'll need to begin monitoring them and checking for the expulsion of the mucous plug," I reply.

"I think that you're in good hands here with Dr. Wolfe, Loretta," says Dr. Kelly.

Loretta laughs loudly and grabs her belly.

"Great job, Dr. Wolfe," she teases.

"Okay guys, we're in the home stretch. This could happen at any time, so I am on a twenty-four-hour call for you," says Dr. Kelly. "Here is my cell number, Mr. Wolfe. Don't be shy to use it, okay?"

"Understood, doctor," I reply.

He exits the room with a wave.

I spend the morning hanging on at the hospital, making calls to update the myriad of interested parties on both sides, reading Tolstoy to Loretta, and chewing the Russian fat with Yev. Loretta doesn't have much of an appetite at lunch, eating only some broth and vegetables. Dinner, however, is a horse of another color.

"Do we have any turkey wings left?" asks Loretta hungrily.

"Why yes, I do believe so ma'am. Would you like me to prepare a plate for you?"

"Yes, please, I'm absolutely starving."

"You should be pretty hungry. You had an okay breakfast and a very light lunch; and then there's that giant tapeworm inside you. I'll get the dinner warmed up."

There is enough for a modest dinner for Loretta, and I eat the remains, with a little gravy. Loretta relishes the home-cooked food even more so than the day it was originally prepared. Fortunately, there wasn't enough food to cause consumption discomfort, just enough to sate the appetite.

I'm feeling worn out for some reason. I haven't really done anything, but I'm tired. I clear the dinner stuff and grab a brownie from a tray near the nurse's station.

"Something sweet, thank you," says Loretta. We settle into a conversation about children that we know, and how different the reality was for their parents when compared to the expectations they had. We talked about her sisters' children, her friend Donna's kids, Nala and Junior, my cousins' children. We spoke of the hope that all parents hold in their hearts, and prayers for their children whispered into the darkness. We wondered out loud about the new light inside her that would soon break into the world. We wondered, and let the weight of that wondering sit there like an object between us.

I turned on the television and settled into some television staring. I wasn't watching, and I was sure that Loretta wasn't watching either. I sat there in the chair next to the bed, holding her hand and sharing the same unspoken thoughts.

"Can I get you anything honey; perhaps a cup of decaf tea," I ask?

"Perhaps a bottle of water thanks," she replied.

Reaching into the fridge, I pull out one bottle and one from the top of the fridge for Loretta, as she cannot abide cold water. I start the nightly ritual that will culminate in sleep by retrieving Loretta's toiletries and getting ready for bed. Sleep comes surprisingly quickly for Loretta, and for that, I am thankful because tomorrow is potentially the biggest day of our lives. I will not sleep though because I need to track those contractions. The fact that we were in a hospital staffed with doctors of every description and nurses of many types has not escaped me. However, I have got to stay on top of this for *us*.

I wander out onto the floor at about 3:45 a.m. to stretch my legs. Walking past the nurse's station, I notice Yev standing outside his wife's room. He looks up and sees me coming toward him, but uncharacteristically, looks back down at the floor. He does not look up as I draw nearer, but pushes away from the wall and turns and takes two steps. I read the body language to mean that we're to walk together so we may speak without being overheard.

"Morning, buddy. You're up late," I say.

"You too," he replies.

"Loretta is has been experiencing labor since this morning," I say opening up.

"Oh shit, Vonstone, it's about six months, no?" he asks.

"Twenty-five weeks and six days, Yev," I tell him. "He's coming, and there is nothing they can do to stop him."

"You seem calm."

"I feel calm, at least for now, Yev. I've been monitoring the contractions and relaying them when the PCT comes in," I tell Yev. "How is Olga?"

"We're up and down, Vonstone," says Yevgeny. "They're monitoring the twins twenty-four-seven now because the heartbeat on the boy was hard to hear."

Yevgeny has clearly not been sleeping, and though we have not seen much of each other, he has been here constantly.

"We're in the right place, Yev. This hospital ushers more than seven thousand healthy babies into the world every year. Obviously, with those big numbers come more than their share of problem pregnancies. As a consequence, they handle more problem and premature births than anyone else. Yev, if you were to have a problem, and I hope that you don't, this would be the place to have it."

"I wish Olga was awake to hear your encouragement, Vonstone. I feel more confident just listening to you, man. Thank you so much."

"I'm only too happy to help, Yev. Listen, I've got to get back. How about some outside breakfast in the morning?"

"That sounds good. We feed the wives first though, right?" asks Yev.

"Only way to go, Yev," I say chuckling a bit as I walk back toward the nurse's station.

When I return to the room, Loretta is snoring like a freight train, which is great, because if she's awake, she's in pain. I sit on the edge of the chair and look at her in the dim light. Her face betrays the fact that, though asleep, the pangs of labor continue unabated. I sit back in the chair and recline a bit, thinking about Yevgeny and Olga, and wishing that Loretta had a chance to meet her, here in this place. Such a meeting might mean a great deal to them both, if it were to happen.

I open my eyes, and Loretta is staring at me over the bed rail. "I'm glad you got some sleep," she tells me. "How much'd you get?"

"About forty five minutes," I say glancing at the clock over the bed.

She winces as a contraction happens. I record the time, the duration, and place the pad back on the vitals station.

"I'm having breakfast with Yev later, across the street at the diner," I tell Loretta.

"That's a good idea. You need a break away from here," she says.

"How about you? When do you get a break away from here?" I ask jokingly.

Of course I know what she means, but I'm in it for the long haul, and I need to reassure her of that fact. "You're here, I'm here, got it?"

"Got it," she says smiling and feeling reassured.

"We're a team, ma'am, and we're getting this done, the three of us, and the three of us are gonna diddy bop outa here one day real soon," I say, my voice wavering a bit, and my eyes welling up.

Loretta's eyes water a bit too, and we hold hands. Just then, the PCT walks through the door, whispers good morning, and begins to do her thing. After taking the vitals, she picks up the pad, tears off the top page, and places the pad back into the basket.

"I'm starving," says Loretta.

"I'm quite hungry too," I reply.

Hearing this, the PCT says, "I think there are some Ensures back there somewhere. Let me go have a look," she says waddling out of the room.

She returns about five minutes later with three Ensures and two glasses of ice.

"Thanks so very much, young lady," I say.

"How far along are you?" asks Loretta.

"About seven and a half months. I have a long way to go," she says suddenly looking a bit tired.

The PCT leaves us with a, "See y'all later," and once again waddles out of our sight.

Loretta finishes her Ensure, rinses, and returns to a sleep posture. I ease back in the chair and recline a bit, feeling much better about Loretta and the contractions.

I step out into the hall, leaving Loretta sleeping lightly and find the shift change in full swing. "*Las manos sucia*" (dirty hands) walks past and shoots me a look, and I give her my Mr. Spok eyes before I go back into the room as Loretta is stirring.

"I seem to be developing some expertise in pissing off PCTs," I joke.

"It appears to be a gift" she replies less jokingly.

"Hey, I drop the hammer where it needs to be dropped, ma'am, with no excuses or apologies," I say as I sit down.

We chit chat for a while I tidy her up. I tell her of my conversation with Yev and how upset and utterly unsettled he felt. Sharing the difficulty that they are having with the heartbeats, Loretta says that she wishes that she could meet Olga. I tell her that I had the same thought. The PCT comes in to change the linens and collect the contraction times. Breakfast arrives, and I arrange it on the table in front of the bed, as Loretta cannot get out of the bed because of the contractions.

"I'm not hungry any more," says Loretta. "What time is your breakfast with Yevgeny?"

"After breakfast sometime," I reply. "Since you're not so hungry, would you like another Ensure?"

"I think so, but no ice though, sir."

"You got it, ma'am."

I open the Ensure, stick a straw in it, and place it on the table. I sit in the chair next to the bed and outline my plans after breakfast. I explain that I plan on going to the bank, home to check the mail, pay some bills, and finish up some sanding in the nursery.

"In the mean time, I'll ask the charge nurse to call me immediately in the event that anything happens," I tell her. "If you feel more comfortable with me staying close, I'll come back after breakfast with Yevgeny."

"Don't be silly, you need to get out for a little while. Go, go right now, okay?

"Okay, I won't be long, ma'am," I say kissing her on the head. "Bye, honey."

As I walk past the nurse's station, I see Yevgeny exiting the room.

"Ready Vonstone," he asks?

"All set, sir," I reply. "Let's go."

We exit L & D, and I show Yevgeny the shortcut out onto 48th street through the ER. There are snow flurries as we exit the ER waiting room and navigate our way through the smokers crowding the exit.

"Buddy, do you mind letting us through?" says Yevgeny to a large bearded man.

The man turns toward us, and I swear, he's got a cigarette butt stuck in his beard.

"Oh my god, that guy's got it bad," says Yev, cracking up. As we enter the diner, which doesn't do a brisk sit down business at breakfast, we head for a table by the window. "I know what I want, Yev."

"Me too; I'm having four eggs, toast, and coffee."

We quickly realize that we need to place the order at the counter, so we move over to the counter and place our order.

"I'd like a ham steak, three eggs, with home-fries, and coffee please."

Yev places his order and quickly tells the cashier that he is buying.

"Thanks, Yev," I respond. We enjoy a relatively leisurely breakfast, sharing gut busting laughter about the stuff we've experienced since being at Maimonides. I share with him my plans for the day as well as my concerns about a spontaneous birth. Yev feeds me my own comforting words from earlier that morning.

"Those are very comforting words, Yev," I say smiling.

We finish up our coffee and walk back outside. The flurries have subsided, but it is bitterly cold. Yev extends his hand to me and says, "Thank you, Vonstone, you are a friend to me."

We shake hands, and for some reason, I say, "See you on the other side, friend."

We walk in opposite directions on 48th Street until I turn the corner onto Ft. Hamilton Pkwy.

The day is smooth and predictable. I get the errands done and check in with the nurse's station in the mid-afternoon, and everything appears to be okay. I finish up the last of the sanding and am in the midst of the cleanup when my phone rings. I see Loretta's number on the CID.

"Hello, ma'am. How are the contr …"

"If you want to see your son born, you'd better get here *now*, because I don't think he's going to wait. They're taking me right now!"

I don't ask a single question, but begin to move as soon as I hear the urgency in her voice.

"I'm there already," I say hanging up and tossing the phone out of the shower onto the sink.

I'm peeling off the dust-caked work clothes in the shower, and washing off the compound dust with which I'm covered. I'm out the door in about four minutes flat. You know it's so funny, one makes all of these intricate plans with contingencies for everything. You plan what you'll need to do, the things that you'll need to take, and the exact words that you'll need to say. However, the moment confounds all those well laid plans, and you're left with the mad dash, and words completely inadequate to the moment. The trip to the hospital takes exactly eleven minutes, and the parking gods are favoring me this evening, as there is a spot waiting for me on Forty-Seventh Street. I race to through the front entrance past the idiot guard who is saying something that I cannot quite make out. I barrel down the corridors, finally making my way to the previously identified delivery room. A familiar face approaches with gown, cap and mask in hand.

"Here, let's get these on you, tiger," says Lynn Hammerhand helping me into the garb. "I told you you'd be seeing me again." She ushers me into the delivery room where Dr. Kelly and a midwife are at work over a surprisingly calm Loretta. The only sounds coming from her are some grunts and hard exhalations.

"Breathe, Loretta, slow in and force it out," says Dr. Kelly.

I get hold of her hand, and she squeezes hard. On the wings of prayer, with a single deep breath, a hard push, and a shrill cry, a bright new light has entered the world. Joshua cries for the first time at 5:16 p.m. on the 31st of January 2005. He is swabbed and presented to his brand new mother for the first time. Loretta looks over at her at her precious boy with tears in her eyes.

"Hello, my baby boy; it's your mommy," she says through the veil of pain.

None of it matters now, not the pain nor the fact that there was more work to be done. She was able to see him, where before she'd only been able to feel him. Hammerhand turns and moves toward me with our newly arrived baby in tow. When I stare into his big eyes, I feel as if I'm suddenly drowning in those big black/gray eyes.

"Hello, my sweet boy. I am your dad, and you are my son forever," I tell my boy.

I thought for a long time what I'd say when I met my son for the first time, but those simple words and tears seem most appropriate.

"I can't believe that he came out crying. I've never seen a preemie just come out and cry like that; I'm absolutely in awe," says Dr. Kelly as Hammerhand whisks Joshua away for weighing, testing, and prepping for the NICU.

"Okay, Loretta, stay with me. Now, we have to do the hard part. There are pieces of placenta still attached, and only way to do this is to put my hand in there to get them out, so hang in there with me, okay," says Dr. Kelly.

Loretta takes a couple of deep breaths in preparation, and Dr. Kelly gets to work. She tries hard to bear up, but when she screams, it rips the heart out of me, and my eyes start to tear. I feel so helpless standing there listening to her scream.

"Oh god, oh god it hurts," screams Loretta as I rush over to her to make my presence known!

I try to grab her hand but its flailing everywhere.

"Oh god it's not supposed to hurt so much," she screams. "Something's wrong!"

I finally get hold of her left hand, kiss it, and press it to my chest.

"I'm here. I'm right here," I shout to her.

"Dr. Kelly, no …" she says as he traps and excises the last piece of the birth sack.

The tears are running down her face and mine now, but it's over; it's really over. Now, it's time to begin the next chapter. This great hero has done her work and done it well, now it's time for "the Light" to take center stage.

CHAPTER 10

THE WARDEN

Loretta is ushered to her new room on the maternity ward, and is promptly given something for the pain that will doubtless overtake her soon. I produce two bottles of Ensure that I procured on the way past the nursing station.

"I knew that you would not wish to eat right now," I tell her.

"You're so right," she says. "What you can do for me though is to …" she start before I cut her off.

"Let me guess, go and check on our son now" I say.

"Yes, leave me, go," she replies surprisingly forcefully.

"I'm going, but I just wanted to see you settled in, honey. You were such a trooper, and I'm so proud of you. I'll return with a full report," I assure her. I leave the new room, which is on the third floor of the maternity ward, and make my way down to the NICU; and for the first time, I walk through the door, which I have only ever passed by, briefly glimpsing any action inside.

"May I help you?" said an imperious looking woman sitting behind the reception desk.

"We've just had a baby, and I am here to visit with my son and meet with the neonatal practitioner," I reply.

She must have sensed my bewilderment because she placed a wrist band on my left hand and bade me go into room one and wait for my child. As I thanked her and walked away, she said, "I've got to go over the rules and procedures with you, Mr. Lawrence, but that can wait until later," says the formidable one.

I step out into the main corridor and begin the short walk to room no. 1. The NICU is comprised of five rooms; room one reserved for the critical care of newborn preemies who will require constant monitoring, the other three rooms step down in severity, and the fifth room is what we call a pumping room, where the moms would go in order to use the breast pump. As I reach room no. 1 and turn to go in, the door at the end of the corridor marked "Authorized Personnel Only" flies open. Two nurses, accompanied by the ubiquitous, Lynn Hammerhand, enter the room pushing a radiant warmer containing the Light of my life.

I stand aside in order that they might pass, and fall in behind the procession into room no. 1. I remain in the background as the nurses attach sensors to Joshua that will enable the room staff to monitor him. I sense Lynn looking at me from behind, but I am transfixed by the light on the radiant warmer.

"Can we talk for a moment, Mr. Wolfe, if you don't mind," she says finally, walking in the direction of the exit?

"Sure, Lynn," I reply following.

She leads me into a room behind the reception desk with signage that says "Parents' Room." Once I'm inside, she closes the door. The room has two chairs, a couch, a coffee table and an end table. The main feature though, is a set of lockers covering two sides of the room.

"Let's talk about the situation that you, your wife, and newborn son are in, Mr. Wolfe. I'm not going to make a big long speech, nor am I going to sugar coat anything for you. You've got a sick baby here, and there are certain things that *you're* going to need to do. He's gonna have good days and bad days, days when you feel like he's ready to go home, and days when you thank God for the NICU. You're gonna watch his weight like a hawk because that is the visible indicator of health and progress, and that too will go up and down. He may need a surgery or two while he's here, but amidst all of that, just keep in mind that his chronological birthdate, sometime in May, if I'm not mistaken, will likely be his discharge date. The ups and downs in his condition will level out by that time, and you'll take your boy home. Your wife may not be good to anybody for three weeks, three months, or more, who knows? So they're gonna need you to be there, for *both* of them. You're gonna need to be there on both ends, at home for her and at the NICU for your baby," said Hammerhand never taking her eyes away from mine.

I instinctively want to talk, to say something, because that's what I do, but I restrain myself, because I want to hear this; I need to hear this. Not necessarily because I haven't played this in my mind a hundred times, but it is an important affirmation of what I need to do, and who I need to be.

Hammerhand goes on, "It breaks my heart when we usher children, vulnerable little ones, into the world, and the parents don't make the commitment to do the things necessary to give the emotional support that's gonna make the difference. We can do great things with science, and we can give nutrition that will sustain your boy physically, but that connection with the parents is absolutely critical, Mr. Wolfe. You'll have to be here because your wife may not be able to for a while anyway because some women suffer from *postpartum depression*. You have to do as much as they'll let you do, in the care and feeding of your boy. As you keep coming around every day, and these nurses get a sense of you, they'll trust you to help care for your son. Be here, be active, be involved, ask lots of questions, and don't be surprised if the moment comes when you'll have to kick some ass. Just remember, you're here for …"

"Joshua," I chime in.

"Thank you, Joshua, you're here for Joshua, not to make friends, so don't worry about anybody's feelings. You've gotta be strong in here, Mr. Wolfe. Do you understand what I'm talking about?"

"I know exactly what you mean, ma'am. Be the present advocate, the observer, the helping hand, and the hammer when necessary, but don't be an asshole about it. Look for allies in the care of Joshua, not friends; is that about right?" I ask.

A smile builds on her face as I'm talking, and by the time I'm done, it's a full on toothy grin.

"I think you're gonna be just fine, Vonstone, just fine. At some point when your wife comes down, I'm going to have a conversation with her as well. It'll be a little different than this one," she says smiling.

"It'll need to be," I respond.

"I got a sense that you needed the unvarnished truth," she says.

"Thanks, Lynn," I say, "just what the doctor ordered."

She smiles flings open the door and leaves the NICU. When I emerge from the parent's room, the lady at the reception desk is laughing and extends her hand.

"Nurse Hammerhand gave you quite the going over, eh? I'm Mrs. Coles, by the way," she says. "They call me *the warden* around here. If you ever need anything in here, come to me, okay?"

"Pleased to meet you, ma'am," I say. "And thank you, by all accounts, we'll be here in your care for quite a while so I imagine we'll be needing lots of help. Why warden?" I ask.

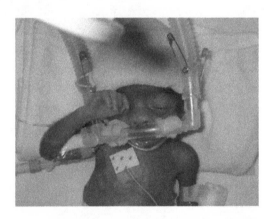

She smiles a wry smile and says, "Because nothing gets past me. I just need to cover some basic NICU rules, Mr. Lawrence. Here's a locker key. The lockers are for storing things that cannot be taken into the NICU; it's for daily use so return it to me, or whoever is sitting here after each use. The sink is for washing up each and every time you enter the NICU. The room behind me, as you've already discovered, is the Parent's Room, and it is for the exclusive use of the parents. It is not a waiting room, or a place to leave older children, which brings me to the next rule: NO CHILDREN IN THE NICU. Do you understand these rules, Mr. Lawrence?" she said finally.

"Yes, ma'am, I do. My name is Wolfe, by the way, Mrs. Coles," I finally correct her.

She smiles that smile again and just nods at me without saying a word. I wash up and walk back into the unit and straight over to where my son is in repose. I examine him carefully for the very first time as he lay in the radiant warmer. Joshua is twelve and a half inches long and about four inches wide at the chest, his head clad in a knit hat to help him maintain his body temperature, was the size of a medium sized navel orange. He weighed in at one and a half pounds, his skin was translucent, and yes, he was the most beautiful baby I had ever seen. I sat next to the radiant warmer for about thirty minutes before remembering that Loretta was awaiting my report. I flash out of the NICU telling the warden, "I'll be back," and was out the door before she could utter a single word.

Finding my way back to Loretta, I enter the room quietly expecting that she may be asleep. I sit down, exhale, and allow myself to relax. *Wow, that was quite emotionally exhausting*, I think to myself. Just as I feel as if I'm about to melt into the chair, I hear Loretta's voice, sounding raspy and tired.

"How's my son?"

"He's good, strong, and appears to be doing well," I report. "There's a shift change happening right now down there, so I'm going back down to have a word with Dr. Petrov, so I'll have more specifics then. How are you?" I ask her.

"Tired, and really, really sore, and hungry," says Loretta.

"I was about to ask about that," I say. "I'm all over it. Let me see what is out there in the hospitality room."

I dash down the hall to the hospitality room where I find two trays untouched. A passing PCT bids me help myself, and examining one of the trays, I find broth, fish with rice, and potatoes and Jell-o. I work a bit of magic by pouring off half of the chicken broth, warming up the remainder, flaking the fish, and adding it to the broth with the rice and putting it back in the microwave for a bit. I grab some crackers and a few cookies and head back to the room where Loretta is awake, but dozy.

"Aren't you glad to be rid of Trendelenburg, ma'am?"

"You better believe it," she says.

As I arrange the meal on the tray, and move to raise the bed, she says, "I miss him."

I wait for the rest and continue to fuss with the bed.

"I miss him being inside me where I could touch him and speak to him." She says, "Now he seems so far away."

I get the food in front of her and uncover it, but she's still looking at me and waiting for me to say something.

"Until you can get there to be close and renew the connection that can never be broken, I will be that unflinching connection," I tell her. "Now try some of this creation."

Uncovering the meal, Loretta says, "Hey, that smells pretty good."

Tasting it she tells me that this is just what she needed, as she scarfs down the soupy mixture, cookies *and* Jell-o.

"Thanks, chef, that was surprisingly good. You've got to doctor up this hospital food more often sir," she tells me.

"The feisty little man came today. Can you believe he cried when he came out? His little engine was already running. He didn't need to be started," I say.

"Dr. Kelly couldn't believe it; he said that he was in shock," replied Loretta.

I drop down on my knees at her bedside, reach over and hug her.

"You did it! You were so brave, so strong," I tell her. "You brought him in," I say suddenly emotional and sobbing. "You did it, you did it … "I say, now completely breaking down."

"Thank you, God, for grace and providence. Bless this little boy, I pray, from the great storehouse of blessings, with strength for the difficult journey that lay ahead. We pour out this prayer into the infinite universe of possibilities, for the best possible outcome for our little boy. We are under no illusion about how hard it will be, or how serious Joshua's condition is, but we know what is possible for those who believe," we pray.

"Amen," says Loretta sleepily.

I lay there holding her until she falls asleep, at which point I clear the dinner service and head for the hospitality room to grab a TFS and some milk. I board the elevator and press "1," and just before the doors, I think I catch a glimpse of Yevgeny, but cannot be sure. Arriving at the NICU, I'm greeted by Mrs. Coles.

"Hello, Mr. Lawrence, you're back," she says.

"Hello, Wardie," I reply.

She laughs out loud, I mean a deep belly laugh.

"We're going to get on just fine," she says still smiling, and I throw a knowing smile back at her.

There is a flurry of activity at Joshua's bay, and I notice that the radiant warmer has been replaced by an isolette. I walk over to the isolette and greet my son.

"Hello, Joshua Wolfe," I say for the first time ever. He is resting in what can only be described as a nest. I introduce myself to the room "1" nurse.

"Good evening," I say to as she is already walking in my direction. She is a petite woman of about thirty, with short cropped hair.

"Good evening, Mr. Lawrence, I'm Nurse Malau. I'm taking care of your son …"

"Joshua," I tell her.

"Yes, Joshua; I'm taking care of him tonight," she tells me. "That makes two Joshuas in this room. Your son's neighbor is also Joshua," she tells me.

I turn to my right to see s plump, amazing looking boy. I stare in amazement, and wonder to myself just why this healthy looking boy is here?

"Looks great, doesn't he?" says the nurse.

I nod slowly.

"There are many reasons that children stay with us, Mr. Lawrence," she explains.

I don't ask, and she never says. He is literally four times the size of my Joshua, no exaggeration. Dr. Petrov saves me the trouble of hunting him down and walks over to talk to me.

"Dr. Petrov, I presume?"

"Yes, Mr. Lawrence," he says hesitatingly shuffling papers to find the parent's name.

Dr. Petrov gives me a plain vanilla assessment of the situation, much like an interviewee who sits there while the interviewer reviews their resume and application, then proceeds to recite the resume when the interviewer says, "Tell me about yourself."

I thank him and make a decision to talk to someone else as soon as the opportunity presents itself. I, like the employer am looking for impressions, subtle insights, and opinions, not the party line. There are a staggering array of valves, instruments, dials, monitors, gauges, and instruments in each bay. Each self-contained bay is designed for the support of a single life; yes, the NICU is a developing marvel.

I made a decision while Joshua was still in-utero that I would expose Joshua to classical and jazz early. When I told my dad about it, he went out and purchased a Disc-man in order to facilitate the effort. I decided that I would make a weekly selection from my vast array of cd's to play for him.

"Hello, little boy; daddy is back here with you. What are you dreaming about, son? Do you recognize my voice from all the talking that mommy and daddy did while you were inside mommy? I think that I'm going to head back upstairs now, son, because I suspect that we'll have to wheel mommy down to visit with you later," I tell my son.

I reluctantly leave my perch to find Nurse Malau to tell her that I'd be leaving, but that I'd be back later; but she's busy lending a hand in another room, so I do not disturb.

"Goodbye, Wardie," I say as I flash past her.

"Gone so soon," she shouts through the flung wide door?

"Oh, you know, *I'll* be back, ma'am," I reply.

Loretta is snoring murderously when I return to the room. Hearing her snore, I realize that though I haven't had the kind of day that Loretta has, all the running up and down has me feeling a little *nappish*. This has indeed been a day like no other. I slip into the bathroom, wash my face, brush my teeth, and change into a t-shirt, sweat pants, and slippers. I slide onto the cot beside the snoring beauty, determined to catch a little nap. Whenever Loretta budges, we'll pay a visit to Joshua. My head swimming with all the events of this day, and thoughts of my new son, I finally surrender to sleep.

My eyes slowly open in the dim light of the room, and the clock across the room comes into focus. It's a quarter after twelve, and I'm suddenly aware that Loretta is awake. She shuffles her legs under the covers when she's just awake, or when she wants to wake me without saying, "You awake?"

"Hey, mister, can we go visit our son?" she asks. I wrench myself from the cot, suddenly aware of just how magnificently uncomfortable the thing is and has been. Stretching until I hear joints cracking, I say, "I know where there's a wheel chair ma'am; I'll be right back, okay?"

"Cool," she says rather excitedly.

I step out of the room and down the hall to a recently vacated room where the PCT told me that she had secreted a wheel chair when I asked for one. Usually, the transportation staff keeps a pretty tight rein on the equipment, numbering, and inventorying them, but I got lucky.

"Your chariot awaits your pleasure, ma'am." I announce as I reel out a few disinfecting wipes from the dispenser on the wall. I give the chair a good going over before gingerly helping her in.

"I feel pretty silly in this thing," says Loretta as we wheel down the hall toward the elevator. "I know I need it though because my legs are so week," says Loretta before I can respond.

We arrive at the NICU, and I back in with the wheelchair. Greeting the night clerk, I show Loretta the parent's room as we pass. I wheel her over to the sink to acquaint her with the procedure, and then down the hall to room no. 1.

The room is dimly lit, and Nurse Malau sat on a high stool doing some paperwork. As we enter the room, she stands, walks over, and reaching out a hand to Loretta, introduces herself.

"I'm Malau," she says in a pleasant welcoming voice.

Taking her hand, Loretta responds in kind, "I'm Loretta, and of course, you've already met Vonstone."

"Yes, and I have a feeling that we'll be seeing a lot of him here in the NICU," replies Malau.

Loretta's eyes invariably find the other Joshua, but she stays on mission. We arrive at our son's isolette and he is as I left him. He stirs slightly and Loretta perks up hopefully.

"Do you think that he knows we're here?" asks Loretta.

"Why don't you talk to him?" I tell her.

"Hi, baby, mommy's baby, mommy's love. Your mommy is here," she coos.

As she looks in at her new born baby boy, I move over beside her and, locking the wheelchair, help her to her feet. Malau is standing by on the other side of the isolette.

"Why are there blankets over the isolette?" asks Loretta.

"Without moving away from my son, or turning around," I answer her.

"According to what I've read they do that for three reasons: to mute the effects of the light, to dampen the sound, and in some cases, counter the effects of a nearby A/C vent that may be blowing on the isolette. It's basically a simple work around because new NICU spaces are constructed for that purpose, as opposed to being re-purposed from other uses," I chime in. Apparently, Loretta looked over at Nurse Malau because I heard her say, "That's right."

I look at Loretta and notice that she was beginning to tire, so I help her back into the wheelchair.

"What's that thing across his face?" asks Loretta.

"Care to take a stab, Mr. Lawrence?" asks Malau.

"It's called a CPAP, and it helps babies whose lungs haven't developed sufficiently to get the oxygen that they need. They can increase and decrease the oxygen as needed, from 100 percent down to the air that we're breathing," I reply.

"Somebody has been doing their homework," says Malau.

"You have no idea," says Loretta. "He is a world class know-it-all, nurse.

"Hey, easy there," I say mounting a playful defense!

We thank Nurse Malau, exit the NICU, and take the long way back to the elevator. "Thanks for taking the long way back," says Loretta, "it's good to be out, if only for a little while.

"I just figured we'd go for a little ride," I say with a smile on my face.

We pass the elevator and go for another turn past the NICU. I see another doctor going through the door of the NICU and recognize that he must be the neonatologist in charge this evening. I tell Loretta that I'd like to speak with him with regard to Joshua, so we hasten back up to the room and get her settled in. She's asleep before I leave the room.

I race back to the NICU and find the doctor in room no. 3.

"May I help you, sir?" asks a nurse.

"Please tell the doctor that I'd like a word in room no. 1 when he has a moment," I reply.

"I will," she says.

I proceed to Joshua's room where I take a seat next to his isolette and wait. As I sit there looking at my son, I have so much to say to him, so much to tell him about what's in my heart. Yeah, I know that he's a baby, but I want to pour out my heart to him anyway. Just then I hear a voice behind me and I turn to greet the doctor.

"Good morning, Mr. Lawrence, I'm Dr. Patel," he says.

He has a warm assuring manner about him, and his eyes are a bit tired.

"Good morning doctor, I'm Vonstone," I reply.

"Vonstone…, that is a very interesting name," he says.

"I try to do it justice doctor," I say ending the brief banter.

"I have a few questions with regard to Joshua's current state, and what we can expect in the days and weeks ahead? I notice that Joshua is fitted with CPAP breathing assistance. What percentage oxygen is he breathing right now?"

"Well right now, Mr. Lawrence, Joshua appears to be oxygenating quite well on room air. The device is merely blowing air into his lungs to help him breathe," replies Dr. Patel. "There are many bells and alarms that go off on that monitor over there. Don't let them drive you crazy because they are meant to alert the staff of conditions that are not necessarily emergencies."

"I know that every premature birth is different, but what are some general expectations with regard to similarly situated premature births?"

"You're correct to acknowledge that we have to be cautious when speculating and generalizing about these little fellows, as each one is unique, but a couple of rules that apply across the board, such as the fact that he will lose a bit of weight in the first few days, but gain pretty steadily after that. Here in the NICU, it's all about the weight. Babies that make the weight and meet some other criteria, get to go home," says the doctor.

At that moment, though behind him, his eyes tried to go to the other Joshua in the room, at which point he looked back at me and said in a softer, almost wistful voice, "Most of the time anyway."

"Thanks for coming over, I do appreciate it. I will doubtless have many more questions as time goes by," I tell him.

"No problem, we're here to help," replies Patel in a reassuring voice as he leaves the room.

"Just you and me kid; you and your daddy. No matter what happens, daddy's *got* you. Whatever goes down in this place, you're going to open your eyes and your *daddy* is going to be right *here*. Mommy and daddy love you more than we love ourselves little boy, and we're here for you, *no matter what*. Daddy is going now, but I'm not going to be far. Mommy and I will see you in a little bit."

He stirs a bit and that brings a big smile to my heart, as I back away and then turn and leave the unit.

I slip back into the room quietly and into the cot, only to hear Loretta ask sleepily, "How's my son?"

"He is great," I reply, "absolutely great."

She lets her hand fall over the side of the bed, and I grasp it, and pressing it to my face I say, "Thank you."

"Look out for him," she says in response.

"I promise."

It has been a day like no other, and sleep has not seemed at all important, or needed. But with thoughts of my newborn son swimming in my head, I surrender and sleep, as always, is the victor.

Rising early after getting only a few hours, I dress and slip out of the room. Passing the nursing station, I tell the charge nurse to inform Loretta that I will be returning in less than an hour. I slip out the front of the hospital and head for the car. It's bitterly cold, but I'm layered nicely. While the car warms up, I send an email that I had queued up last night while in the NICU, to a select few people informing them of the birth of Joshua Wolfe. This was informational, but more so to trigger the avalanche of prayers that will see us through this time.

I "backroad" my way home and enter this peculiar place. I empty the bag of dirty clothes, replacing them with fresh ones in the event that I need to stay another night. Loretta had already requested her discharge outfit, if that was to be today. She wanted something loose fitting and easy to put on. The purple jumpsuit with an off-white tank. *Perfect*, I think to myself. And we'll need a pair of flats, and her long black coat.

I slip upstairs to the music room and grab the CD player that my dad had bought for his new grandson. Moving over to the CD cabinet, I select Brahms, Coltrane, Debussy, Mussorgsky, Marsalis, and Parker. "That should do for now," I say out loud. Even with morning traffic, I make it back to the hospital in an hour. I've missed shift change, so I head for the parking garage, but before I can turn in, I realize that the parking space, which I had left, is once again mine. *How the hell?* I think to myself. Not being one to look a gift-horse in the mouth, I pull in, and none too soon, as a familiar nemesis eyed the choice spot hungrily.

Exiting the elevator, my phone begins to ring, and it could only possibly be Loretta. I walk into the room with it still ringing on my waistband. She bursts out laughing.

"What's in the bag, mister?" she asks inquisitively.

"Clothes for you, in the event that you are discharged, and clothes for me in the event that you are not," I tell her. I know what's coming.

"So, let me see what you brought for my discharge outfit, sir," she says.

I plough into the bag and show her what I brought. I get an approving nod on the outfit, but a wrinkled nose for the shoes.

"I don't want to hear it, your feet need something with support but roomy enough to accommodate feet that haven't seen shoes in a month," I scold. "Don't worry about the fashion choice right now. Besides, the jumpsuit legs are so big that your feet will not be seen."

She smiles broadly and says, "You've thought this out quite carefully, haven't you?"

"Yes, yes, I did," I reply.

"Knock, knock," says a voice at the door. It's Dr. Kelly paying an early morning visit.

"Come in, Dr. Kelly," I respond.

"Good morning, good morning. How are you feeling this morning," he asks. "You're not mad at me are you, Loretta, after I caused you so much pain, but we had to get those pieces of placenta out of you, or there would have been serious consequences."

"I understand, doctor, but understanding it doesn't help my soreness right now," quips Loretta managing a smile.

"I did stop in to see Joshua a while ago. I have to tell you, I am absolutely amazed that he cried on delivery, and that he's on room air."

"Room air, what does that mean?" asks Loretta.

"Oh, I haven't had the opportunity to catch you up on everything. If you'll permit me doctor, this part of a more lengthy discussion that we must have," I tell the doctor.

"I'll leave you to it then," says the doctor. "Glad you're doing so well Loretta. Let me know if you need anything."

"Thanks, doctor," I reply.

I begin relating the details from my discussion with Dr. Patel, and all the information that I gleaned. She listens wide-eyed like a child hearing a good story.

CHAPTER 11

SPRUNG

As I began the morning cleansing ritual, the PCT comes in to get Loretta ready for the day. She asks if I'd like her to take care of it, and I say, "Okay," after glancing at Loretta for approval.

"I'm going to take this opportunity to go down to the birth registrar," I say.

"Good idea, then we can go down and visit my son."

"Sounds like a plan, ma'am. I don't know how long it takes, but I imagine that there are only a few forms to complete, so I'll be back in about fifteen or twenty minutes,"

I assure her as I walk out the door. As I exit the room and turn toward the elevator, it occurs to me that I have not seen or spoken to Yev since breakfast yesterday. I silently hope that he, Olga, and the *tvins* are doing well. I make a mental note to call his cell later.

Completing the forms and handing them back to the clerk who smiles and says, "Joshua Olivier Matthias Wolfe, that's one hell of a mouthful, sir," prompting a smile in response.

"How much of you is in there if you don't mind me asking?" she says still eying the lengthy moniker.

Handing her my driver's license, I say, "In the name, a little, in the boy everything."

The clerk clenches her mouth, her eyes suddenly softening as something, on the page before her, catches her eye. She nods at me slowly with a knowing smile playing around her mouth, and finishes me off with a stamp and a soft, "Thank you and, good luck."

I retreat slowly, as if backing out of a royal audience, with a thank *you*. As I turn, I walk right into Nurse Hammerhand.

"Good morning, Mr. Wolfe. How is everything this morning?"

"Everything is great. I am actually on the way up to get Loretta to bring her down for a visit."

"This a good time for that talk?" says the nurse.

"No moment like this moment, ma'am. We'll be back down in about fifteen or twenty minutes if all goes well," I tell the nurse practitioner.

"Excellent, I'll swing back in about thirty?"

"Perfect, we'll see you then," I agree.

Back in the room, Loretta is dressed, ready to roll, and looking positively radiant.

"You look terrific," I tell her. "What did you do since I left?"

I mean it, she looked really good.

"I need a haircut *badly*," she shares pulling both hands back over her hair, but unable to resist smiling that trademark smile.

"They're discharging me tomorrow."

"When did that happen?" I ask, quite surprised.

"Dr. Kelly was just back here and said that he thinks that there is no reason that I won't be able to go home," she says with mixed feelings playing out on her face.

"You're going to miss it here," I joke.

"Going to miss being close to my son, you mean," she chimes in quickly.

"Of course, and speaking of whom ..."

"Let's be off," I say. "The wheelchair is right here. The nurse recommends that you walk a bit, ride a bit, okay?"

"Got it," she says as I help her ease into the chair.

I wheel her right up to the door of the NICU where she eases out of the chair and gingerly walks in on her own steam.

"Mr. and Mrs. Lawrence, good morning," says Mrs. Coles.

Loretta looks at me with a wrinkled brow but says nothing.

"Good morning, Wardie; how are things?" I reply cheerfully. Loretta shoots me a look at hearing me refer to Mrs. Coles as *Wardie*. Mrs. Coles catches the look and laughs.

"It's okay, Mrs. Lawrence, we have an unspoken understanding, your husband and I," she says with a broad smile.

Loretta smiles, washes her hands, and starts through the door into the NICU, when Nurse Hammerhand walks through the main door. They exchange pleasantries and disappear into the Parent's room. Oh to be a fly on that wall …

We pass a pleasant visit with our son in room one and meet the nurse in charge, Nurse K. She was much older than the other nurses that I'd thus far met and seen in the NICU. She spoke haltingly, slowly, and though competent I'm sure, did not inspire confidence, at least not in me. So, right or wrong, I was always watchful when she was on shift. While taking care of the other Joshua, that big, healthy *looking* boy who was our Joshua's neighbor, she commented that he had been with them a while.

"This Joshua has been with us for a few months now," she said. "The other babies they come and they go, but he is still here. He is the *grandfather of the unit* right now. There will be another long resident, but right now, it's Joshua."

When she spoke about him, her voice was a bit sad because I imagine she had a good idea of what the issues were. I never did, and never sought to know.

"What do you feel like having for lunch, ma'am? How about some red pea soup?"

"Mmm, that would be perfect. You know that I never turn down red pea soup."

"How was your chat with NNP Hammerhand?" I finally ask.

Loretta looks at me, shaking her head.

"She's a little negative for me. I mean, she kept referring to Joshua as a *sick baby*, but you know I don't see him that way."

"I know you don't," I reply. "What else?"

"She encouraged me to take my time and heal; not to be in a rush to establish routines, but get lots of sleep and get used to being back home. Focus on healing physically and mentally she says. She tried to tell me that I may not be able to get back to the hospital for a while, first physically, but later mentally. I don't know what you said to her, but she thinks that you're fully capable of holding it down here, so I shouldn't worry. What did you say to her anyway?"

"I guess it's more of what she said to me, and how I took it," I reply.

"Well, I'll rest up for a day or so, but after that, I'll be back here to visit my son," said Loretta.

"Yes, ma'am," I reply with a smile.

We had several conversations about post-partum depression, and the devastating effects that it has on many women. I do not, however, think that my superwoman believes that this will in any way apply to her.

The soup is delicious and just what this moment called for. After clearing the dinner paraphernalia away, I step out into the hall to place a call to Yevgeny. I am a bit concerned for their absence from the hospital, and the staff cannot ethically provide me with any information. The call goes directly to voicemail. I relate my concerns about them to Loretta.

"Give them some time," she says. "Sometimes, people need a little space."

Of course she's right; she usually is for that matter.

"I'm going to go home tonight. I really feel as if I haven't lived there much in the last month. If you're to be discharged tomorrow, I'll need to make some preparations, particularly shopping, cleaning and laundry," I tell her.

"Agreed. What time will you head out?"

"Soon. I want to stop by my folks and catch them up on the latest details, but I'm going to drop by ShopRite, on my way there, for the groceries."

"I am so looking forward to being back in my bed," says Loretta.

Darkness has fallen, and I detect rain on the window.

"Would you like me to take you down again to see the little man before I leave?" I ask.

"You really read my mind you know," she replies.

"I'll get a chair," I reply. "By the way, how is the pain?"

"I feel like someone stuck their hand up inside me and pulled my insides out. Oh that's right, they did."

"I'd laugh if it weren't so serious."

"Well, I'd laugh if it didn't hurt so much," she shot back.

I wheel her down, and we spend almost an hour with our son, after which I take her back upstairs and put her to bed with CNN.

ShopRite is busy as expected. It is not unusual to find it so at midnight. I grab the basics with plenty of fruit and veggies, making a mental note to swing by the butcher to get some oxtail for Sunday's dinner. I call the folks, on my way to the car, to make sure that they'll be home when I get there. The roads are slick in the light drizzle as I make my way through the side streets. Arriving in the driveway, I spot my Ma'Dear standing at the window looking out, anticipating my arrival. She disappears from the window, and the door opens moments later.

"Hello, my son," she gushes hugging my neck.

"Hello, *grandma*," I reply.

"I've waited so long to be called that," she says.

"Well, ma'am, the wait is officially over," I tell her smiling.

I hear my dad coming briskly up the stairs from the basement.

"Good evening, and congratulations, sir," he says giving me a big hug. "Would you share a celebratory drink with me?"

"Absolutely," I reply.

We all sit at the kitchen table, and I bring them up to speed with all of the latest information from the NICU, and Loretta's pending discharge. I partake in some of the banana fritters, which Ma'Dear has just made, as they pepper me with a thousand grandbaby related questions. Happy grands.

Our house has not been lived in or had, or what Ma'Dear likes to call, the breath of life in it for some time. Ma'Dear maintains that this is what causes an otherwise healthy house to die. I queue my house cleaning playlist, put away the groceries, and get started with the cleaning. I wrap up at about ten thirty with fresh linins and flowers I picked up at ShopRite. I shower, make a Chivas and ginger, and go sit in the family room and relax with an old school jazz playlist.

As I'm really getting into Lester Young, the house phone rings, and I answer. "Hello?"

"Mr. Wolfe, how is everything?" queries my cousin, Patrick. "I just drove past your house and noticed the lights on for the first time in a long time."

I'm usually in the family room with some soft lights listening to music.

"Everything is fine, all things considered. Loretta is being discharged tomorrow morning, and I've been busy getting the house in order," I tell him.

"How is Joshua fairing?" he asks.

"My son is holding his own. He is a tough and determined little man; qualities that will doubtless serve him well in life." We chitchat for a bit as I provide him the details of the past twenty-four hours, and he listens and provides some valuable context for the hospital dynamics. Patrick actually graduated from NYU Medical School, and on the advice of his mentor, took some time off before his residency. The time off was to have been spent establishing a financial foundation in real estate, which would make the residency somewhat less taxing. This was in the early eighties, and things must have gone quite well because he never quite started that residency.

"Mr. 'P,' I've got to go. We'll talk tomorrow when everything settles down, okay?"

"No problem. Give my regards to Loretta."

"Will do; later," as I sign off.

I am tired in earnest, and the only thing on my mind are those tightly tucked sheets that are going to feel so good against my skin. I place calls to Loretta's key people to apprise them of the details about Loretta's release, giving only basic details regarding Joshua. I instruct them to wait to hear from her, if she's feeling up to it, and in any case, not to wear her out with long conversations. If she was not feeling up to it by day two at home, I would call with updates. Sleep comes quickly, and I know this because I don't remember a single thing after setting the alarm on my phone.

"Good morning, sunshine," I say as Loretta's eyes open.

She raises her head and looks around, appearing a bit confused. I sense her disorientation and help her out.

"You're still in the hospital, ma'am," I tell her.

She rubs her eyes and smiles.

"How did you know?"

"You looked as if you didn't know where you were for a moment," I reply.

"I dreamt that I was at home, and I just got back into bed after going to the bathroom."

"Soon, we'll be home soon, okay?"

"They've been wonderful here, for the most part, but I can't wait to get back home," says Loretta.

"I know. Sleeping at home last night felt strange, but I was so tired that that it almost didn't matter," I report.

"I hope you weren't up all night cleaning," she admonishes.

"No, just a couple of hours. I was done by ten. The nursery is done and ready for paint and carpet. I've selected a color scheme that you'll need to take a look at."

"What's that smell?" she asks.

"Goodness, I almost forgot, I brought Starbucks for breakfast," I tell her finally.

Her eyes light up at the prospect.

"That was a really important detail to overlook, mister," Loretta scolds with a mock frown dancing across her brow.

"Decaf," I say un-bagging the coffee and pastry. "You'll need to start pumping as soon as you get home, if for no other reason, to relieve the pressure on your udders." 'She looks for something to throw at me.

"What's the color scheme that you have in mind for the nursery?" she inquires, relishing the decaf French vanilla and croissant?

"Sky blue walls, with clouds, birds, and airplanes. There will be a yellow sun, and inside the yellow sun will be painted, in glow-in-the-dark paint, a crescent moon, which will only be visible at night."

The ceiling will contain all of the constellations visible in our hemisphere, made with glow-in-the-dark stars and dots."

"Wow," she says. "You've put a lot of thought into this, haven't you," she says sounding quite impressed.

"I imagine laying on the floor of the nursery with him, looking up at the ceiling, and pointing out the constellations in his night sky, and having him develop an interest, knowledge and love of the heavens. I've been dreaming too," I tell her.

"Wow," she says again.

"Oh, and did I mention that I've redone the closets?"

"Which ones?" she asks.

"All of them," I reply.

"Where did you find the time?" she says with a combination of amazement and alarm.

"You *have* been in here for a month," I reply. "And I haven't been at the gym nearly as much as I'm accustomed."

"I'm really impressed," she says.

"I took all the measurements and decided on cedar paneling and shelving. I also have a friend from the gym named Humphries, working at Home Depot who gathered all of the required materials for me. Patrick, who also knows Humphries since his house is next to a building Patrick owns on Thirty-Ninth Street, picked them up for me and left them in the house, even placing the right amount of materials, more or less, in the rooms where they would be needed," I explain. "That saved me a whole lot of shopping and carting time to and from Home Depot."

"That's so awesome that they were able to help that way," she says.

"Now, would you like to freshen up to go down and visit our son?"

"Yes, I thought that you'd never ask. I think I'd like to walk, though, okay?"

"Excellent. I'm so glad you're feeling up to it," I tell her. "But we'll take it slow, and we'll have the chair along just in case, okay ma'am?"

"Yes, doctor," she quips.

The very instant that Loretta lays eyes on Joshua, she says, "He looks smaller," and indeed she is right. Without checking with the room nurse, I can see it too. Nurse Kay comes walking over to us and says, "Good morning, Mr. and Mrs. Lawrence."

"Good Morning, Nurse Kay," I reply.

"At what point are you going to let it be known that your name is not Lawrence?" Loretta asks, almost sounding a little annoyed.

"I did mention it to Mrs. Coles, but the next moment she called me Lawrence again. I think that this is a way to connect me to my son, and that's okay."

"Will they change the name on the isolette?" asks Loretta.

"To my understanding, this will not happen during his stay here," I reply.

We spend about an hour in the presence of the *light*, not really saying anything, just sitting there watching. Occasionally, he would make some movement, and we'd smile. Loretta slides from her stool and moves over to the isolette. Placing both hands atop the unit, she began to silently pray. I stand, move over to the opposite side placing my hands atop hers, did likewise.

Returning to the room, the nurse was placing something in Loretta's chart.

"This is it, Ms. Lawrence. They are discharging you this morning," says the nurse.

"Hallelujah," says Loretta.

"Not that we don't appreciate all that you've done for her here, but it's time," I tell the nurse.

Laughing, she replies, "We took good care of you to make this day possible."

As the nurse departs, Loretta begins getting dressed in preparation for the anticipated discharge.

CHAPTER 12

THE WEE SMALL HOURS

There is an absolute boundless glee with which Loretta awakens to find herself in her own bed. Every time that her eyes open and she realizes that she is *home*, a look of satisfaction comes over her face. She is stretching making the stretching noise as I walk through the door.

"Morning, sunshine," I greet her.

"Morning, honey. What time is it?" she asks.

"The time is 9:30 a.m. and all is well with the world, at least the portion of it that concerns me," I tell her.

"How is my son this morning?" she asks. "I know that you called," she says smiling.

"You're right, I did call at six before the shift change, to find out how he passed his night, and Nurse Betty in room no. 1 said that he was *pretty fine*, but was a bit vague on the details, so I'm going to get you some breakfast and head over to the hospital to get more information."

"You're not going to make a pain of yourself, are you?" asks Loretta.

"Absolutely," I reply. "It's what I do, my dear."

We both share a good laugh, and I head into the kitchen to prepare her breakfast.

"Good morning, Wardie!"

"Morning, Mr. Lawrence. You're way too cheerful this morning," she says.

Washing my hands, I enter the unit and am immediately greeted by a tall angular man in blue Maimonides scrubs.

"Good morning, Mr. Lawrence I presume," he says. "I'm Dr. Gollisano, the director of the NICU."

"Good morning, Dr. Gollisano, I was hoping that I'd run into you at some point."

"Well, here I am. Do you have any questions or concerns that I can address?"

"Well now that you mention it, I'd like to make it known that more information is better for me than less. When I call for a status, I only expect vanilla to the extent that the report is vanilla. Otherwise, I expect spumoni, if you get my meaning."

"Details, you want the details, right?"

"Exactly, we understand one another splendidly, doctor," I reply. "This is how my brain works; it assembles details into a narrative. Anything left out creates a hole in the narrative, and it doesn't make any sense. Do you understand what I mean?"

"Yes, I do. I'll make sure that you get the details that you require, Mr. Lawrence."

"Just between you me and Mrs. Coles, the name is Wolfe," I whisper.

Smiling, the doctor asks, "Then why is everyone calling you ..."

"I allow it because Lawrence connects me to my boy. He is Boy Lawrence and Baby Lawrence, no matter what his birth record says. So, you see, it's less complicated that way."

"I get it," says the doctor nodding.

"Now, in the spirit of this new understanding, what is it that the nice nurse was not telling me?" I ask.

"Okay, we have been monitoring what appears to be a murmur in Joshua's heart.

"Do we know what is causing this murmur?" I ask.

"Yes, there is a canal between Joshua's aorta and left lung, called the *ductus arreriosus,* which is essential for life in-utero, but harmful to his respiration once out of the womb. The canal should close within a few days of delivery, but in Joshua's case, the canal remains open and is interfering with his ability to maintain effective respiration. It actually did show signs of closing, but suddenly and spontaneously dilated. Medication will usually close the canal, but failing that, surgery will be necessary," explains the doctor.

"Understood. What medication will you give him, and when will the course begin?"

"We typically use a medication called indomethacin to close the canal, and we can begin as soon as tomorrow morning," he says.

Dr. Gollisano cautions, however, that indomethacin has side effects; therefore, Joshua's urine output and stool quality will need to be monitored constantly for any sign of the side effects.

"Okay, let's make it happen as soon as possible doctor. Thank you, I will inform Loretta immediately."

I slap my hip to retrieve my phone and the doctor moves off to resume his mission.

The first of the three doses was administered this morning with good results. The sound of the murmur is diminishing by late afternoon, indicating that the canal is closing. A second dose will be given tomorrow, followed by the completion of the course on Friday morning. Joshua's heart rate and respiration are much more stable (and mine as well), though I've received the general operating principle of the NICU to the parents of all residents receiving treatment, *don't expect too much too soon*.

Loretta has been spending long hours sleeping, and Ma'Dear has been visiting daily and preparing nourishing soups and porridges for her. Our wonderful neighbor, Gianna (Jeanne), has been great with the little baked treats that Loretta enjoys so much. It has been an enormous load off of my mind to know that Loretta has company and lunch when I am out. Sleep, as NNP Hammerhand pointed out, is the tonic for the physical and mental healing. I am also happy that she's not driving herself crazy with every detail of Joshua's care.

Joshua's heart rate is less erratic, and mine along with it. He is passing a quiet night as Dr. Patel comes over. I turn to my head slightly in his direction and smile. No words are spoken; he just stands there for a few moments, puts his hand on my shoulder, and then is gone.

"Joshua, my son, it's raining cats and dogs outside, and your daddy is quite tired. I'm going to leave you with some music that I hope that you'll like. It's by a composer named Antunin Dvorzak. I hope that it gives you as much pleasure as it does your daddy," I tell my boy.

Cleansing my hands, I take the sterilized Discman from the Ziploc bag, and place it inside the isolette pressing play. As I back away, blowing him a kiss, an image of a boy of seven or eight curled up in a comfortable chair, reading plays in my mind.

Loretta is wide-awake when I get home and in the mood to hear details. I shower, jump into the bed, and pour over the events of the day in great detail. Loretta has a hundred questions, and I answer them in great detail knowing that I am the only conduit for information related to Joshua. She was particularly pleased hear that the PDA was showing signs of closing. I continue sharing until alas I can stay awake no longer, and allow the warm, healing waters of sleep to wash over me at last.

Morning comes so quickly these days, and I awake to the gentle patter of rain on the side of the house.

Coffee, I need coffee. I head for the kitchen to make breakfast and dial the NICU as I walk. They have just administered the second dose of indomethacin without incident. I whip up a couple of omelets with sliced avocado, toast, and coffee. Loretta hears the commotion, and I hear her heading for the bathroom. After a couple of minutes, she comes into the kitchen.

"Morning, something smells really good," she says.

"Good morning, honey. I do hope you're hungry because I've made a big breakfast. Mascarpone cheese and scallions omelet, with avocado, toast, and coffee," I tell her.

"Where do you dream this stuff up?" she asks.

"You're exactly right. I do literally dream of things that I think will taste good. I dreamt of the mascarpone cheese and scallions a couple of nights ago," I reply.

"Damn, this is so good," says Loretta. Did you call the hospital yet?"

"Yes, I did, and they have administered the second dose of indomethacin. I will have a better idea of any impact on his urine output when I visit later."

"Good breakfast. I do love the taste of my own cooking," I tell her.

"Hey, could you make me another omelet, minus the toast this time?" she requests.

"Be happy to, ma'am," I reply.

Loretta relishes the omelet, and I delight in making it for her. Cooking for people and having them enjoy what I prepare is truly a passion of mine. Loretta, however, is in a special category because she is what I call my worst critic. If something is not up to my usual standard, I will hear about it from her. She doesn't sugarcoat anything. She has told me in the past that "this is the worst thing that I've ever had from you," so I feel confident that if she says it's good, then it's good, and if she raves, well then it's likely otherworldly good.

It's a stellar morning in the *garden spot of New York*, the rain having given way to the sun, so instead of driving to the hospital, I head for the bus stop on the corner. I meet the two neighbors closest to the corner, engaged in conversation.

"Morning, neighbors," I say cheerily.

"Vonstone, good morning," says Jeanne.

"How is Loretta this morning?"

"She's well, and in good spirits. We've just enjoyed a delightful breakfast together, and now I'm on my way to the hospital to visit with my son," I tell her.

Before she can ask, I rattle off the menu, causing her to erupt in girlish laughter. Jeanne loves to hear such culinary details.

"Love to Joshua, and please be sure to stop when you get back because I baked last night," she says, a cherub-like smile crossing her face.

Loretta absolutely loves her goodies, and she like me loves to have others enjoy them.

"Why don't you stop by and visit with her awhile? She'd love to have your company for a bit," I say as I spot the bus stopped at the light and jog to the corner to catch it.

Jeanne nods and says okay as I round the corner. Once on the bus, I call Loretta, letting her know that Jeanne will be calling to schedule a visit.

The ride to the hospital is pleasant and refreshing as it is a rare occasion for me to be in a vehicle that I'm not driving. I take the opportunity to queue up a couple of emails and do the thing that I love to do the most in New York, people watch. I don't mean celebrities or athletes, because about that ilk I could care less. I mean real people, the kind you see on a bus, train, walking down the street, or arguing on a corner.

There's a fender bender about three blocks away from the hospital, and I ask the driver to let me out so I can walk the rest of the way. As I exit the bus on this lovely, brisk New York morning, I feel the gentle cold on my cheeks as I walk the remaining couple of blocks. The ER entrance is too quiet, and I need chaos in order to be able to slip confidently past distracted and beleaguered guards, so I head up the hill to the main entrance.

"Good morning, Wardie," I say greeting the gatekeeper.

"Mr. Lawrence, good morning," says Mrs. Coles, briefly breaking away from some unpleasant gatekeeper duty before her, and then returning immediately to the task before at hand.

I don't stick around to be nosey, though I must admit to being tempted. As I turn the corner to make my way toward room No. 1, I see Dr. Petrov about to enter room No. 3.

"Good morning," he says somewhat uncertainly, as if gauging a response from me.

"Good morning," I say quite definitely.

He keeps on his way, and I do not press the questions in my mind as I have already received a report. Moving into room No. 1 and passing by Joshua's enormous namesake, I sing a greeting to my son that I will sing to him for years to come when waking him.

"Good morning to you, good morning to you, good morning dear Joshua, good morning to you. And how are you today?" I think he recognizes my voice, because he kicks a few times.

"Yes, it's your dad. I am here to be with you son," I tell my dear boy.

Just at that moment, Dr. Petrov enters the room and moves toward us.

Walking to the other side of the isolette, he says, "Mr. Lawrence, the indomethacin is having its desired effect on the PDA, however, the monitoring of the urine output revealed that it was down sharply. Therefore, I have decided, in consultation with Dr. Gollisano, to push back the last dose in the course for twelve hours."

"Understood, doctor. How long can this dose be postponed before the effect of the last dose becomes moot? In other words, I guess I'm asking, if the PDA can reopen, and leave us without pharmacological options?" Petrov stops for a moment and looks at me carefully.

"I researched indomethacin doctor," I tell him.

He smiles and tells me that the shorter the interval that passes between doses of indomethacin the better. A twelve-hour postponement of a dosage is not bad, but we would not be able to postpone the final dosage again and would be forced to cancel that dose and hope for the best.

"Because of the harmful effects of the indomethacin, the course cannot be repeated. In the event that the closure should be incomplete, or reverse itself, the only remediation would be surgery," says Dr. Petrov.

"How likely is that scenario to unfold if we are unable to complete the course?" I ask.

"Sad to say, it is more likely than not. We could see complete closure with the two doses already in, but that is not a likely outcome. The odds favor an incomplete closure or a reversal of the existing progress."

"Thank you, Dr. Petrov."

I spend the remainder of my visit talking to my son and playing Nat King Cole, Dizzy Gillespie, and Lester Young for him. The whole time, all I can think about is returning to the poor oxygen saturation of a couple of days ago.

Loretta is becoming physically stronger with each passing day. Her mental state, though, is another story. Hammerhand had made a suggestion to me and told me that I would know when to put it into action. I think that now is the time to promulgate this phase of the process. Looking at her sleeping, she startles me by suddenly raising her head.

"What the hell?" she says. "What are you looking at? What time is it?"

"It's three-thirty," I tell her, laughing a bit as she checks for drool.

"Why are you up? Are you having trouble sleeping?" she asks.

"I'm looking at your boobs," I tell her.

"They're not for you; they are for Joshua," she says.

"Well, I'm glad that you said that because it's time to start pumping that wonderful milk out of those magnificent boobs." She nods her head in agreement.

"We'll start tomorrow then, and it'll be every four hours around the clock, okay?"

"Okay, now can we get back to sleep? Milk cows need their rest, right?" she jokes.

"Yeah, but that doesn't start until tomorrow, so for now. I just want to make sure that everything works."

"You're going to make a mess," she says.

"It's only milk, honey, and I promise not to waste a single drop."

The completion of the course did not happen last night, and my morning call revealed that the urine output remained unacceptably low. It has been fully thirty-six hours since his last dose of indomethacin, and because the effect of the drug is cumulative in the system, the passage of thirty-six hours is too much time without the third dose to make it effective. Miraculously, however, the PDA has closed as confirmed by a chest CT, rendering the final dose unnecessary. The doctors continue to express concern over Joshua's low urine output, but all are justifiably happy with the overall result.

"I think that we can live with that, right? After all, no one said kidney damage, they're just watching it," says Loretta somewhat pensively.

"We're in a good place, make no mistake. The PDA closed with two doses as opposed to three, and the drug temporarily slowed the function of the kidneys just a bit. I think that we're sitting pretty ma'am," I say reassuringly.

"That's what I feel as well," she says lending agreement.

Looking at me from the side as I sat on the bed, tilting her head, waiting for me to turn and face her, Loretta said, "It's time."

I look back at her smiling and nod in the affirmative.

Loretta attires herself splendidly, as only she can, and we presented ourselves at the NICU together for the first time since she was discharged.

"Good morning, Mr. and Mrs. Lawrence," says Mrs. Coles cheerily. "It's good to see mommy and daddy here together."

Loretta shoots me a slightly puzzled look that only I can discern. "Just roll with it," I tell her.

"Good morning, Mrs. Coles," replies Loretta.

"Wardie," I reply.

"How are you feeling?" asks the Wardie.

"Quite well actually, a bit tired, but … oh you were referring to Loretta then?"

Everyone laughs, and Loretta reports on her general health. As we move to wash our hands, who should walk in but NNP Hammerhand.

"Good morning, folks. And so it begins. Don't forget what I told you about kangaroo care," she whispers with a wink.

"We won't," we say almost together.

"Thanks so much," I say.

Hammerhand's *Irish eyes* are truly smiling as she disappears into the bowels of the NICU.

We both walk into room no. 1 and notice that the parents of the other Joshua are present. Looking up for a moment, the mom smiles slightly, her eyes misty and red from crying. Her husband, with his hand on his wife's shoulder, never looks up. We proceed over to our son's isolette and greet him.

"Hello, Joshua, mommy's baby. Mommy and daddy are here, baby."

Squeezing her hand and kissing her head, I leave them alone to begin the critical bonding process, and so it begins indeed. I walk out of the NICU and down the hall to the gift shop to purchase three 33L bottles of water for storage in the locker. The cool, dry environment of the NICU engenders great thirst. In addition to that, I'm about to gather a pumping kit for Loretta to begin the process of gathering the life-sustaining milk that Joshua will require once off of the current TPN regime (*total parenteral nutrition is a thick yellow liquid, resembling urine, that is fed intravenously, bypassing the gastro-intestinal system. Containing all the nutritional requirements, it is given to virtually all preemies at one time or another*).

Loretta has put in three solid hours of mommy time in the NICU today. She has pumped, cooed to her son, and talked to the nurses and doctors. It has been a good and productive day, but she is beginning to visibly tire and is doubtlessly hungry.

"You look tired and hungry," I tell her.

"I had a good visit," she says. "Thanks for leaving me alone with him."

I smile.

"What do you do when you're here?" queries Loretta.

"I do pretty much what you're doing, minus the cooing of course. I do sing to him though. It's mostly about maintaining a presence to make sure he knows that I'm here and that all that should be done and observed, is," I tell her.

"The nurses," she asks, sounding a bit alarmed?

"Rarely, according to what I have observed. Those women are superheroes, and an absolute marvel to watch. It's mostly ancillary support people like phlebotomists who pose a problem and bear watching," I report.

"What do you sing to him?" she asks me.

"Well, mostly Nat Cole," I tell her. "I think that it might become our thing."

"Tell me what you know about the phlebotomists," says Loretta, sounding concerned.

"When you spend as much time in that room as I do, you almost become a piece of furniture. This young phlebotomist came in, laid down her stuff, put on her gloves, and proceeded to touch everything in the immediate vicinity. Just as she reached for the isolette, I asked, 'What are you doing?' 'I'm just going to draw a little blood,' she said."

"I don't think she saw me or had any idea that what she was about to do was in any way problematic. I asked her not to proceed and sent an immediate email of complaint to Joshua's patient advocate."

"Wow, what the hell happens when nobody is watching?" says Loretta, sounding quite alarmed.

"I made a decision the night that manos sucias (dirty hands) came in to take your vitals that I'd have to spend, more hours than might seem rational, watching over our son," I tell Loretta. "It is what it is, ma'am. It was not the first incident, and I am certain that it will not be the last. It's just par for the course."

We rise together, and Loretta prays over him, and all the children in the NICU, and we conclude our visit, pausing to glance back at our son resting peacefully, as we leave.

CHAPTER 13

SOLITUDE

Loretta's breasts are positively engorged with milk, and I have a timer that beeps every four hours to remind me to set up the pump. Even 2:00 a.m. is not too ungodly an hour to milk them. Our freezer is becoming quite full of four ounce bottles of milk. I relish my duties setting up the pump and attaching it to her boobs.

"You're having way too much fun there, mister," says Loretta, her voice dripping with faux admonition.

"Only trying to be helpful, ma'am," I reply adjusting the pump and switching it on.

She smiles with her eyes closed and the motor on the pump begins to whir softly. The bottles fill quickly, and I lingeringly clean her up while she sleeps; and being wide-awake; I get up, dress, and, leaving a note on my pillow for Loretta, head for the hospital.

My early morning drive to the hospital is quick, and it's about 4:00 a.m. as I find a parking spot. I park about a block away and walk up the hill to the hospital's ER entrance. The guard, whom I have become quite familiar with, is tired and distracted as usual, and I wave, put my head down, and move through the door into the inner sanctum of the ER. Carroll, the nightshift gatekeeper, is shocked as I enter the NICU.

"Good morning, Mr. Lawrence," she says looking quite surprised to see me walk in at 4:35 a.m.

"Hello, Carroll, top of the morning, young lady," I remark.

Carroll always has such a pleasant disposition. She works the desk at night while going to school during the day for something or the other. The nurses, on the other hand, are never surprised when I show up. With them it's kind of a double-edged sword because on one hand, their charges thrive with parental interaction, and that is good for everyone; but I present as somewhat of an interloper, robbing them of some of the intimacy and freedom they might otherwise enjoy. I have learned to accept both edges of that sword, and I am becoming adept at working them.

"Mr. Lawrence, when do you sleep?" asks Joshua's room nurse.

"When I can, my dear, when I can," I reply.

Joshua has gained twenty-five grams in the past forty-eight hours and is visibly bigger than a week ago. These little milestones mean a great deal to a preemie parent, as we count down to the day we'll be able to walk out with our sweet boy. His feeds are up to 7 mls, and continue to increase by 2 mls daily.

"How is my boy doing tonight?" I ask the nurse as she reenters the room. As I ask the question, I move around the isolette and fold back the blanket used to filter the light. I notice his color to be perceptibly off.

"We took a blood culture about two hours ago and sent it off to the lab," she says.

Before I can begin the assault of questions, she retires to call the attending. About five minutes later, Dr. Shah enters the unit and finds me performing my A&D therapy on my son.

"I think he likes it," says a familiar voice entering the room.

"Good morning, Dr. Shah," I reply. "I understand that a blood culture was taken a little while ago. I noticed that his pallor is a bit off this morning. What do you suspect?"

"As you noted, his color is a bit off, his abdomen is somewhat distended. and respiration, as a result, somewhat elevated. We suspect that he may have an infection, and so I've ordered the culture. We should have the results back within twenty-four hours, Mr. Lawrence," says Dr. Shah.

"Is NEC suspected, doctor?" I ask pointedly.

NEC (necrotizing enterocolitis) is the bane of every preemie parent's existence. It is an infection of the lower intestine charac-

146

terized by the death of parts of the intestine. The only treatment is surgery to remove necrotic tissue and antibiotics to help stem the tide of the infection. Even if everything goes right, surgically, NEC has a 50 percent fatality rate, so for this reason, no NICU parent wishes to hear the words, "We suspect NEC."

Shah thinks for a moment and says, "It is almost certain to be some kind of infection, which is why we started the vancomycin course, but I don't think NEC, but we have to rule it out."

I realize that for *hope's* sake he has put himself way out on a limb. An unreasonable person, with a mind toward litigation, may have had the wheels start to turn, but I appreciated those words more than I can say.

"Thank you, Dr. Shah; you'll let me know the instant the labs come back?"

"We certainly will, Mr. Lawrence," replied the doctor.

I immediately retrieve my phone from the locker and step out to call Loretta with an update.

"Hello," says mommy, sounding remarkably awake for this time of the morning.

I fill her in on the details of my conversation with Shah.

"How does he look?" asks Loretta.

"His color is a bit off, and the abdomen is a bit hard and distended," I tell her. "You know that I like to see his oxygen saturation in the nineties, right? Well, it is in the high seventies right now, and the attending has taken blood labs," I report.

"Is there some sort of infection," asks Loretta?

"According to Shah, based on his general condition and appearance, it is likely to be some variety of infection, which is why they started the vancomycin," I reply.

"Is there any possibility that it's NEC?" Loretta asks rather cautiously.

"Shah all but dismissed the possibility, and I feel pretty good about it as well," I assure mommy. "As you might imagine though, I am somewhat concerned about the desaturation episodes. No one told me this, but I think that this is largely due to the hardness and distention in his gut," I speculate. "I'll raise it with the attending in a bit."

"You staying there awhile?" she asks expectantly.

"Yea, I'm going to tarry for a bit, so rest assured," I comfort.

"Good, keep me posted," says the general.

As I acknowledge her and ring off, I notice two young men rounding the corner coming from the L & D waiting room. The one on the left is incredibly tall, perhaps 6'8" tall, and the other 5'4" or so, the difference in height made more so by the act of walking with a giant. I'm sipping my water and scrolling through missed calls on my mobile as they approach. I overhear the tall one telling his friend in an impossibly deep voice, "And this is the NICU where a specially trained staff of nurses and doctors care for preemies. I was a preemie and began my life in a place not unlike this one," he tells his friend.

"Can we go in there?" asks his diminutive friend.

"No," he almost scolds, "That is not permitted. They maintain tight infection control in there."

"Gentlemen," I say greeting them.

"Good morning, sir," they say simultaneously.

Addressing the tall one I say, "Forgive me, but did I overhear you telling your friend that you were a preemie?" I ask him.

"Yes, sir, I was born at just over three pounds," he volunteers. "Do you have a child in the NICU?"

"Yes, my Joshua resides in there," I tell him.

"If you don't mind me asking ..." he begins before I cut in.

"Six hundred and ninety-five grams," I chime in.

"How much is that?" asks his companion.

"A pound and a half, wow," he says with a quick calculation. "He's a miracle!"

"How is he doing, if I'm not being out of place?" he asks rather cautiously. "My name is Antun, by the way, and this is Brigham."

"I'm pleased to make the acquaintance of you both,"

I say shaking their hands firmly. I take a page from Loretta's book and reply, "Joshua is doing great; he couldn't be better. As a matter of fact, if he were three pounds, they'd spring him tomorrow."

It didn't matter how our son was actually doing; he could be having the worst day, when anyone would ask, she always said that he was doing wonderfully. Her exact words always were, "Joshua is wonderful, you know." She'd make sure that anyone that she spoke with came away with the impression that her son was whole and perfect.

I remember coming home and telling Loretta about how badly Joshua was desaturating one afternoon. Some time later, coming out of the shower, I hear Loretta on the phone, and I know instinctively that she's on the phone with her friend, Pammie.

"Joshua is absolutely wonderful," she was saying.

No matter what was going on, she was not putting anything negative out there with regard to Joshua.

I had an over powering desire to learn details of this young man's life, so I asked, "If you'll indulge a new preemie dad, what are you doing in your life at this time?"

I was astounded and mightily impressed to learn that he was a double doctoral scholar at Columbia University. Wanting to return to the NICU and having held up these young men long enough, I bade them both farewell, thanking them for taking the time.

Brigham replied, "Believe me, sir, the pleasure was all ours," as Antun smiled broadly and shook my hand.

As I walk back inside and smile at Carroll, I perceive a peculiar look in her eyes, but chalk it up to her being tired. Walking back into room no. 1, I find that my son has been intubated. His little body would jerk slightly with every oscillation of the ventilator.

"I know that it doesn't look good, but it is the best thing for him right now," says Dr. Gollisano.

"You're in early," I reply. "I know that intellectually, doctor, but I can't help but dwell on the imagery."

"Let's give the vancomycin a couple of days. I know that he'll respond well," assures Dr. Gollisano.

"We know that he will, doctor. He will because he must, thank you, doctor."

I whisper a prayer into the universe for my boy and depart for home. The morning is crisp and damp as I make my way down familiar side streets past still dark windows and shuttered storefronts, all except one. The house is quiet in the early morning, and I'm greeted by the smell of freshly ground French vanilla. The coffee maker gurgles at me as I enter the kitchen and place fresh hot pastries on the island.

The laptop on the kitchen counter was calling to me. After my conversation with Antun and Brigham, I was eager to search for preemies in history that have done great things despite their early birth. After a very short search, and surprisingly little effort, I was floored at the names that were revealed. It seems that some of the most brilliant minds and accomplished personages in human history were preemies. Napoleon Bonaparte, Isaac Newton, Albert Einstein, Charles Darwin, Winston Churchill, Sidney Poitier, Victor Hugo, Pablo Picasso, Michael J. Fox, Mark Twain, Stevie Wonder, and the stellar list goes on and on. I couldn't wait for Loretta to wake up. I was almost dreading telling her that Joshua had been intubated, but now I had a great story to tell, of my meeting Antun the giant, and the curiosity that gave rise to my new discovery.

"I'm awake," says a voice from the inner recesses of the house.

I pour two cups of coffee as I hear her making her way into the bathroom. By the time she finds her way to the kitchen, the pastry is warm on a plate and the coffee ready.

"Good morning, mommy. Did you sleep well?" I query.

"I fell back into a very deep sleep after I spoke to you," she replied.

And the question that always loomed came next.

"How's my son?" she asked peering at me with those piercing eyes.

"I've got good news, and great news," I begin. "Which do you want first?" I tease.

She smiles and opts to take the news in reverse order. I begin by telling of my meeting with Antun, and follow up with my discovery some of the greatest minds, and most accomplished people in history have been preemies. She is fascinated and encouraged by this news. Then, looking at me somewhat curiously, I sense what's coming.

"And the good news?" she asks somewhat pensively.

"The good news is that Joshua's oxygenation is now perfect, and I've been assured that the vancomycin will arrest the infection. We should have a different picture in a couple of days. However, in order to take the pressure off of his little organs, they've intubated him," I say, ending my brief report.

"How is that good?" she replied.

"Well, it is only one component of the overall process," I tell Loretta.

"Go on," says Loretta.

"Well, they've taken labs to rule out the dreaded NEC, started the antibiotics to deal with an obvious existing infection, and intubated him to take the pressure off his little heart and lungs. Right now, he is working really hard, and is desaturating as a result. The less time that his little organs spend struggling to maintain respiration, the more energy his body can direct toward the healing process. The optics, of him on the ventilator, are not very good, I'll certainly admit, but the plan is sound. There are two downsides that I can see: firstly, his feeds have been suspended until the infection resolves itself, and secondly, the ventilator is good, but the longer he remains on it, the greater the risk of damage to his airways," I conclude.

Loretta is quiet after I finish the report. I know that she's taking it all in and will doubtless have many questions later. I'm starting to feel the tide of sleep rising. Keenly aware of this, Loretta orders me to the shower. I put the dishes in the dishwasher, tidy up the kitchen, and head for the shower. When I make my way back to the bedroom, Loretta is already in bed. I join her, and we stare at one another across the pillows for some minutes until I feel myself surrendering to the sweet majesty of sleep.

CHAPTER 14

A LITTLE MOZART

The vancomycin accomplishes its purpose with deft effect, and the infection, which was determined to be something other than NEC, is vanquished in a matter of a few days, and Joshua is once again looking himself. Dr. Petrov has promised to restore his breast milk to him in another day or so if his progress remains steady. This is great news for us because you see Loretta is an amazing and prolific producer of breast milk. She says that it runs in her family as her older sisters have all demonstrated this prowess.

"Which attending is on today?" asks Loretta.

She knows that I have my favorites and that I have made a note of the rotation.

"Rashdie," I say with certitude as we arrive at the emergency side of the hospital for an afternoon visit.

Loretta is looking a bit uncomfortable as she exits the car and I assure her, "Don't worry we'll get you hooked up to a pump pretty quickly."

She kinda looks at me and rolls her eyes.

"You'd better because you don't want me to start leaking," she jokes, as we both have a laugh.

I typically maintain a dated rotation of milk, transporting the earliest dates frozen in a cooler. I have a supply with me today, and as we arrive in the NICU, I place the cooler near the fridge and get Loretta set up in the pumping room. I return to the fridge in room no. 4 and removing Joshua's milk tray, begin discarding all the milk there. I wash and dry the tray, open the cooler and begin loading bottle after bottle (nine in all) of frozen milk. At that very moment, a new mom returning triumphantly from the pumping room holding a four-ounce milk bottle in her hand with perhaps an ounce of milk inside.

She pauses and looks at me handling the minor mother lode of milk and remarks to one of the nurses, "Is all of that milk for one child?"

"Yes," replies the nurse. "One lucky child."

"Indeed," replies the woman, somewhat dejectedly.

Joshua is regaining much of his vigor. Everyone is happy to see the feistiness return. It is amazing how resilient these babies are. They bounce back stronger each time, no matter what is thrown at them. Loretta returns from the pumping room with four full 4oz bottles in hand. The new mom's jaw hits the floor with a clank as Loretta deposited them in the cooler. She remarks within her hearing that she would have done more, but couldn't bear to be away from her son another moment.

"Showoff," I whisper sharply, as she smiles wryly.

We both head into the room no. 1 to see Joshua and find him awake and alert.

"Hello, baby," says a gushing Loretta. "Mommy and daddy are here."

"Looking good, baby boy," I say. He is a nonstop ball of motion, whether he is awake or asleep. The doctors say that this is the primary reason why he hasn't gained weight at a quicker pace. He's burning up too many calories doing tai chi.

The vital signs monitor catches my attention almost immediately. Joshua's oxygen saturation is not what one would expect, and I slip away to chat with the doctor, leaving Loretta to visit. I ask the nurse if Dr. Rashdie is anywhere about and she says, "No, but let me page him."

As she leaves the room, she almost bumps into Rashdie coming in.

"You're scrutinizing his saturation again, aren't you, Mr. Lawrence?" says Dr. Rashdie smiling.

I'm beginning to get to know a bit about you, I think.

"Yes, I was, and noticed that his oxygen levels are reminiscent of the pre PDA closure levels," I remark.

"Yes, that's right. I'm ordering some imaging, but I think that it's safe to say that the PDA has experienced some level of reversal," says the doctor.

"You mean that it has reopened," I ask.

"That's the theory, though we need the imaging to confirm it. As we discussed before, we get only one shot at it with the indomethacin. After that, surgery will be required to close it, but we need the imaging to confirm the diagnosis," says Dr. Rashdie rather matter-of-factly.

His manner, I suspect, was not meant to trivialize the procedure, but to assure me by suggesting routineness.

"Because he has previously had the indomethacin for the PDA, and vancomycin for the infection, we absolutely cannot go back to a course of indomethacin. Both medicines exact a heavy toll on the kidneys so that leaves us only with the surgical option," says Dr. Rashdie. "There is a remote hope, however, that the complete resolution of the infection which caused the spontaneous reopening, will result in the closing of the PDA, but this is a very remote possibility."

"My great hope was that we would not return to this place, though I understood that a spontaneous reopening of the PDA was a distinct possibility. When will the imaging be done?" I ask?

"We're on the schedule. They could be here at any moment," he said.

"Thank you, doctor, and excuse me, I've got to get back to the room right away," I said rather urgently.

Though the mobile imaging machine would have escaped my notice coming in, I didn't wish it to surprise Loretta without me first bracing her with the details of what was to come.

"I understand," said the doctor knowingly.

I race back to the room where Loretta is chatting up a storm with her son. I pause for a moment and watch her as I realize that Joshua's arms and legs are moving and his eyes are open. This is quite a moment for mommy. I have experienced it before, but I don't believe she has.

"I've been trying to ignore the alarms on the monitor," says Loretta.

"About that, I've just spoken to Dr. Rashdie, and he suspects that the reason for the poor oxygen saturation is that the PDA has reopened because of the infection," I begin. "Because of the use of the indomethacin, and vancomycin, which both impact the kidneys, the PDA issue can no longer be resolved using medication," I explain.

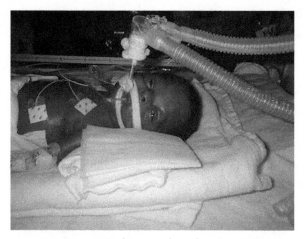

Joshua intubated

"What then …?" asks Loretta.

"At this point, surgery is the only option," I tell Loretta.

She looks at me for a longtime, just sitting there blinking and staring at me. I look back into her eyes, but say nothing, because there is nothing to be said and nothing to be done. I reach out for her hand, and she clasps it tenderly and looks away into some other space. There is no sense of desperation felt between us, but resignation as to the next necessary step.

Loretta and I enjoy a quiet dinner at home, and she doses off with her head in my lap in the middle of ET.

"Was I snoring?" she asks.

"What, you? Never," I make my standard reply.

"I'm going into the shower," she says sounding quite tired.

"I'm coming to watch," I reply excitedly.

"Suit yourself sir," she says laughing.

We each shower, and I get her off to bed where she falls asleep almost as soon as her head hits the pillow. I'm glad of this because she needs the rest. I, on the other hand, am not so lucky and about an hour and a half later, I'm once again in the car, headed for the hospital.

The NICU is quieter than I can remember it ever being. I greet a couple of nurses and move into room no.1 where I notice that my son is not in his accustomed corner. Malau walks over with a big smile and informs me that Joshua has graduated to room no. 2. Apnea episodes notwithstanding, and based more on his milk consumption, and weight, they have stepped him down in critical care.

"Thanks, Malau," I say returning her smile, and as I move quickly to room no. 2, I notice that Joshua is awake and moving around.

"Good morning, mister. Did you think that you could hide from your dad?" I ask him.

I am quite heartened that this relative progress necessitated his move to the next room. This was progress in a very real sense though the apnea continues to be an issue. I sterilize my hands and forearms before reaching into his isolette for the Discman. I've selected Mozart for the evening's entertainment.

"Hey, mister, are you hungry because it's time for dinner," I tell my son as I see Malau come into the room with his feed.

I continue to talk to my wide-awake son as he takes all of his feed, after which I read him some A.E. Housman (A Shropshire Lad) as he doses off. I turn on his Discman and begin to write in his crib side journal where I record all the details of his stay here in the NICU.

I'm enjoying a positively delightful visit with my son tonight. We're sharing Mozart and Housman; this is perfect, absolutely perfect. It's now about ten minutes to two, and I'm feeling a bit thirsty, so I step out to the locker to retrieve a bottle of water. I stop for a few minutes to catch up with Carroll out front before heading back into room no. 2. Walking back into the unit, I notice a nurse excitedly running into room no. 2. I pick up the pace, and when I arrive in the room, Shah and the nurse have Joshua's isolette tray pulled out and are feverishly working over him. As I hasten over, I ask, "What happened?"

"Joshua's heart stopped," replies Shah.

"Would you kindly step out into the Parent's Room, Mr. Lawrence?" asks another nurse as I walk through her to my son.

As I make my way to the isolette, she starts to ask again, and I cut her off.

"Lady, if these were *your* child's last moments on earth, where would *you* be?" I snap.

"Get him a gown please," says Shah rather emphatically!

I slide in on the wall side of the isolette, away from the action and don a pair of gloves. Putting a little A&D ointment on my finger, I begin to massage Joshua's little foot.

"Hello, little boy, your daddy is right here with you. Daddy's got you, my son. You stay with daddy, because I'm not going anywhere."

"We've got him back. Keep talking to him, dad," says the doctor.

I begin to sing, "And now the purple dust of twilight time, steals across the meadow of my heart. High up in the sky the little stars climb always reminding me that we're apart. You wander down the lane and far away, leaving me a song that will not die. Love is now the stardust of yesterday, the music of the year gone by," I croon.

The team has done its work and been effective. Joshua has been revived and is breathing on his own, so I hesitantly leave the room to update Loretta on recent events.

"Hi, is everything okay?" asks Loretta as she answers the phone,

Pausing for a moment, because I know that I need to get this out in one breath I reply, "Everything is okay now, but about a half an hour ago, Joshua's heart stopped."

There is nothing for a few unbearable seconds, and then she replies.

"But now he's okay?"

"Yes, he has been revived, and he's breathing on his own," I reply in my most reassuring voice.

"Okay," says Loretta. "You'd better get back now."

I struggle with her response for a moment. It wasn't anything that she said, or how it was said so much, but the lack of questions. I rush back into the room and sat with my son, switching over to Vivaldi on his Discman. I become aware that the staff is preparing for their shift change. I was clearly so engrossed in updating the daily journal and listening to Vivaldi with my son that a few hours slipped by unchecked.

Placing my hands upon the isolette, I whisper a prayer into the universe, tell my son of our love for him and slip away. Loretta is sleeping when I get home, and I undress and shower quietly allowing the cleansing water to wash over me for a long time. I walked into the nursery to find Loretta's prayer cloth spread on the floor. I knew that she had been praying, but when I stepped over the prayer cloth, I became aware just how hard that she'd been praying. There was a wet spot of tears where she knelt and her head lay.

I walk into the next room and lay next to her on the bed. Without looking up, Loretta says in a small voice, "How's my son?"

"He's more than holding his own," I reply sliding my arm around her waist and pulling myself toward her.

She hugs my arm tightly and pushes back into me.

"Our boy is going to be just fine," I tell her and pull her even closer.

CHAPTER 15

DUCTUS ARRERIOSUS

We've known for some time that surgery is the only option for closing the ductus and creating a pathway toward consistent respiratory health. Additionally, it will remove the steady stress on the heart that could lead to failure. Since the episode of a few nights ago, Joshua has been the focus of intense monitoring. So when we got the call from Dr. Rashdie telling us that they felt that there were no obstacles to performing the surgery at the earliest possible date, we were positively ecstatic.

"When did they say that they'd do it?" asks Loretta excitedly.

"Rashdie said that they'd do it at nine-thirty in the morning on the ninth, yes, that's right, tomorrow," I tell her.

"Another hurdle to overcome," replies Loretta.

"This is just another step toward getting him home, my dear."

The phone rings and Loretta guesses that it's my folks.

"Hello," Loretta answers. "Oh, hi, mom," as she nods at me smiling, then quickly acknowledges my dad as he picks up an extension.

I listen as she gives them the latest details related to the newly scheduled surgery. Someone, probably my dad, obviously indicates that they'll be there because Loretta agrees and says that maybe we can meet for breakfast beforehand. Loretta, having dutifully taken care of the important updates, hands me the phone.

"Hi, Ma'Dear, hi pop; how are you both doing this morning?" I ask.

"Well, the surgery is scheduled, I hear," says pop.

"We will be there, of course," says Ma'Dear.

"Your grandson would expect no less," I chide as they both laugh.

"Absolutely," says pop emphatically.

"Ivey Bell sends her love to you all, and especially Joshua," says Ma'Dear.

"Thanks. How are Ivey and Stanley Bell doing anyway?" I ask.

"They're doing well, but I have a list of prayers and well wishes from friends and family, too long to get into now," says Ma'Dear.

"Well, Ma'Dearest, here is a project for you. Are you ready for this?" I ask.

"Yes, anything for my family," says Ma'Dear.

"I need you to write down each prayer, affirmation and hopeful wish, along with the name of the sender, on a 3x5 index card, and place them in an envelope with Joshua's whole name on it," I explain.

"I'll help with the stationary," says pop.

"Great, then Loretta and I will place the envelope inside Joshua's isolette in a sterile Ziploc bag. In this way, all of the prayers and well wishes will have found their way directly to Joshua. How does that sound?"

"That is a wonderful idea. We'll get started right away," says Ma'Dear.

Loretta, sitting next to me at the kitchen island, nods in silent agreement.

Sleep is not coming easily tonight. I think that I dozed off at about ten-thirty, but it is now twelve-forty-five, and sleep has given me the slip. I lay awake blinking at the textured ceiling and listening to the white noise of the humidifier, and yes, Loretta snoring. My mind is wandering wildly into the past when the snoring lady and I met on the Independent and the myriad of things that could have precluded that meeting and this moment from happening. I think of the moments where I could have been more, done more in our relationship. I look over at her and shed a tear for my occasional thoughtlessness to the snoring wonder beside me.

I think of my son in his isolette, alone, and find at last, the final straw. I am out of the bed, into a pair of jeans, and out the door in five minutes flat. I look at my son as if I haven't seen him in a month. Popping Miles into the Discman and sit down next to the isolette. I wake up just before shift change to "Someday My Prince Will Come." I laugh to myself, bid see-you later to Joshua, and head out.

Breakfast is ready when Loretta wakes up at about a quarter to eight, goat cheese, and scallion omelet with bacon bits and coffee. Breakfast brings a smile to her face upon entering the kitchen.

"What time did you get up?" asks Loretta.

"Oh, about one-thirty or thereabouts," I reply.

"What have you been doing all this time? Please tell me that you didn't go visiting," she says quite knowingly. I smile without answering.

"Order up," I shout and we both crack up.

We present ourselves at the hospital at nine am, and Ma'Dear and pop walk in not long after.

"Good morning, folks. How are you this morning?" I ask.

"Good morning, son, good morning, Ms. Loretta," says pop.

"Good morning, family," says Ma'Dear.

Loretta moves forward to hug them.

"Do we know anything yet; are we still on schedule for nine-thirty?" asks pop.

"We only just arrived ourselves, pop," I reply.

"I would be shocked if there wasn't some delay, pop," adds Loretta.

And as if by some serendipitous happenstance, Dr. Patel walks in behind us.

"Good morning, I had hoped to run into you," says Dr. Patel strolling into the unit.

"I was hoping to run into you as well." I introduce him to Ma'Dear and pop.

"Let me guess, surgery has been pushed back," says Loretta.

"I think you've been around here too long," jokes Patel.

Because we're doing the procedure at crib-side, we're having a resource issue and will need to push back to twelve-thirty," he tells us.

"Okay, that's not the end of the world. We'll be here; we're not going anywhere," I tell the doctor, and with that, Dr. Patel thanks us for our patience, smiles, and withdraws.

We all sit in the Parents' Room, Ma'Dear reading LSF devotional, pop doing his Soduku, and Loretta on the same page in her book for twenty minutes.

"Can I get anyone anything from the gift shop?" I offer. "I need to walk for a bit."

"I'll have some coffee," says pop.

"I'll have one of the blueberry muffins," says Loretta.

"I'll walk with you," adds Ma'Dear.

"Okay, we'll be right back."

We walk out and go in the opposite direction from the gift shop. We stroll and chat for about twenty minutes, talking about family, and old times. Ma'Dear and I do that quite a bit. We've sat together in the backyard swing for hours, just talking about old times and family. We finally turn for the gift shop to fill the orders. I pick up a USA Today, doubting that I'd ever do more than browse today.

"How's everybody doing?" I hear, suddenly jumping awake.

It's Patel, and I have clearly been sleeping for some time.

"We're almost ready for your boy," says Dr. Patel.

"Thanks, doctor," replies Loretta.

We all rise and go move onto the unit. The surgery is actually being done in room no. 1 because it is the largest room. Joshua is awake and being prepped as we enter, and they give us a moment with him. We pray over him for a few minutes, and he never takes his eyes off me as he holds onto my pinky.

"Mommy and daddy got you little boy," I issue through my imaginary psychic connection. Finally managing to tear myself away, I join the family in the Parents' Room to wait.

"The nursery looks great," says mom.

"Thanks, mom," says Loretta. "Daddy did a great job."

"I heard from Patrick and Lor this morning. They want me to let him know the instant Joshua is clear," I tell Ma'Dear. "Would you like to do the honors ma'am?"

"I certainly would," responds Ma'Dear.

I walk over to the locker and grab a bottle of water. I offer, but there are no takers, so I drink alone. The atmosphere in here is quite dry, and I always have a thirst on. I drink about half of the bottle, retrieve my journal, and return to my place beside Loretta, who is busy reading. Pop is working on his Sudoku, and Ma'Dear is engrossed in a word jumble, so I settle into my chair and begin chronicling the events since last night, into this morning.

We four sit just that way for almost an hour, commenting occasionally on things that come to mind. Ma'Dear and I are in the middle of an exchange about best wishes and prayers from aunt Loris and several others when the door opens and the surgeon pokes his head into the room.

"May I come in?" he asks.

"Yes, please, doctor, by all means, do come in," I reply as everyone looks up at once.

"The PDA has been successfully ligated, and in fact turned out to be quite routine. Of course, I don't mean to trivialize the procedure by any means, but everything went as expected, and the PDA is closed without complication. Your boy came through like a champ. All the open PDA complications should begin to subside pretty quickly within forty-eight hours for sure. But I must caution you, of course, against expecting too much too soon. He'll have a fine incision under his left armpit, where we went in, but it will fade over time," reports the doctor.

"What is he doing now?" asks Loretta.

"Well, in addition to the meds for pain, we're going to keep him under until about this time tomorrow. This will allow the healing to begin, absent all that moving around for which I've heard he's famous," says the doctor with a chuckle, and with that, gets a laugh out of the room.

"May we sit with him awhile?" I ask.

"Absolutely, just give the nurses about ten minutes to get him situated. Someone will come out to get you, okay?" he says smiling genuinely.

"Thank you, doctor," we reply.

"Good luck then," he says as he vanishes from our midst.

We all hug and breathe a sigh of relief as we await the all clear. About ten minutes later, the nurse from Joshua's room pops into the Parents' Room with the thumbs up.

We all walk purposefully down to room no. 1 where our charge lies in repose with his eyes covered against the light, after his ordeal. We take up positions around the open bed, in which he is installed, and settle in for a visit.

"How's mommy's baby," coos Loretta, her voice almost a whisper? Ma'Dear and pop beam down lovingly at their grandchild while I move over behind Loretta and place my hands on her shoulders.

"Well, this is the beginning of great things, now that this obstacle is out of the way," says pop.

We sit in relative silence for about an hour until I move over to Joshua's bedside.

"You were born to the right family, my boy. There is no shortage of love here," I tell my son, almost in a whisper.

Sensing the moment, everyone moves closer to the bed and join me in touching some part of it. After a few moments, Loretta begins to pray spontaneously and prays a prayer for the ages, leaving family and staff, within earshot, misty-eyed. Having sat vigil, visited, and prayed, it seemed the right moment to bid our sleeping angel farewell. So we each in our turn, step forward, say a few words, and exit room no. 1.

"See you later, Wardie," I say as we pass the front desk and go out.

"Is anybody hungry?" asks pop in his inimitable way.

"Is there anywhere nearby to get something to eat?" asks Ma'Dear.

"What are you in the mood to eat, mom?" asks Loretta.

"I could eat a whole fish," says Ma'Dear, causing everyone to burst into spontaneous laughter because Ma'Dear is not known for putting away large quantities of food, no matter how delicious.

"There's a Thai/Chinese place not too far from here. I think it's over on 8th Ave," I tell them.

"Sounds good," says Loretta haltingly, looking at Ma'Dear and pop for agreement.

"Let's go, I could eat a lobster," announces Ma'Dear.

"What happened to the whole fish that you were threatening, Ma'Dear?" I ask.

"You never know, I might eat them both," she replies.

"That, I would like to see Rosie," answers pop.

We use one car and drive to the restaurant where Ma'Dear does indeed order the big red snapper, does a pretty good job with it, and washes it down with a crème de menthe.

This early dinner is delightful and relaxing. Pop and I have our usual scotch and ginger, and we all share a decadent desert with four spoons. The topic of conversation turns sharply to our precious boy in room no. 1.

"When do you think that they'll restart him on breast milk?" asks Loretta.

Ma'Dear and pop perk up and look at me. By now, we all understood the relationship between mother's milk and his physical growth.

"Based on past suspensions due to infections or suspected infections, I think that it'll be a couple of days. But the doctors, as always, caution us not to expect too much too soon," I answer.

We wrap dinner and ride back to the hospital where Loretta rides home with Ma'Dear and pop while I head for ShopRite to pick up a few groceries.

CHAPTER 16

SWEET MOTHER'S MILK

It's been a week since the surgery and Joshua is looking decidedly better. His color is much improved, and he is breathing much easier. His life sustaining mother's milk has been restored to him and he is tolerating the milk, and the fortifier they add to it very well indeed. Joshua is gaining weight daily and gets a 4 ml increase every twenty-four hours.

Sitting here watching him is almost like watching someone doing Tai Chi. He will occasionally open his eyes, look at me, and make my heart flutter. Joshua has attained 1485 kg (3.4 lbs.), and is starting to fill out nicely. The nurses have encouraged us to bring in an outfit for him to wear and take pictures on Mother's Day. Loretta has busied herself shopping for the right outfit, fitting for our micro-preemie son. Mother's Day will be an exciting time for her and everyone.

Grandma is seventy-three today and is thrilled that she will get to hold her only grandchild for the very first time.

"Hello, Ma'Dearest," I say as she walks in.

"Hello, my son. How are you and my grandson doing today?" replies Ma'Dear,

"Your grandson is waiting for you. I'm told by Nurse Malau that you'll be able to feed him today," I tell her. Ma'Dear smiles broadly and says, "Really?"

"That's the word in the room, Ma'Dear," I tell her excitedly.

Mother was radiant as she gazed upon her grandson and mused on the prospect of holding him for the very first time. The room nurse came in to set up an area next to Joshua's isolette where Ma'Dear can commune with her grandson.

While I watch Ma'Dear and Joshua enjoying one another, the back door to the NICU opens, and a newborn bed emerges into the passage. Hammerhand and another staff member, whom I do not recognize, guide the bed through the door, followed by the young father. He appears almost to be in a state of grief as I step into the passage and our eyes meet. As the NICU staff receives the new arrival, I approach the dad from the right, and, without a word, place my hand gently on his right shoulder. Upon the merest touch, my young brother turns, buries his head in my shoulder, and the tears come. The raw emotion of the moment envelops the room, and the staff is not immune. Hammerhand delays her departure, pausing at the front exit of the NICU to observe the scene. She catches my eye, and I detect a faint smile, and approving nod as she exits the NICU.

The young man gathers himself.

"I'm sorry," he says.

"There is no need for apologies among brothers," I reply.

"Samir," says the young man extending his hand to me and smiles warmly.

"Vonstone," I reply, extending mine. "Samir, I know that this a lot to take in all at once. Was your wife admitted previously?"

"No, she was rushed here this evening when her water broke. This cannot be good," said Samir, with a fair amount of trepidation in his voice.

"No, Samir, I'm going to be quite honest, there are risks and dangers everywhere for our little ones, but NICU staff know what they're doing," I assure him. "My son, Joshua, was born at twenty-five weeks, six days, and he's doing wonderfully under their care."

Samir's eyes are beginning to glaze over, so I wrap it up.

"Like I was saying, it's a lot to take in, but perhaps when settle down a bit you, and I can sit down and talk as brothers. I think I can help, Samir. I've been here a while, and I know some things that may help you and your wife get through this difficult time," I tell him.

His eyes start to well up as we both stand and exchange a warm embrace.

"Thank you, my brother. I would welcome any insight that your experience can provide," replies Samir, visibly appearing more relaxed.

"Go be with your loved one, Samir," I say as he rises, bows slightly with his right hand over his heart and departs.

Finally, it appears that our NICU experience may help another family after all. I drift back over to Joshua's isolette, and, opening one of the portals, begin to share the details of my encounter with the newest resident of Maimonides NICU. Ma'Dear has dozed off on the other side of the isolette and wakes as I place my hand gently on her shoulder.

"You could be docked for falling asleep on the job, ma'am."

"Just you try it, I think that my grandson may have something to say about that, sir," says Ma'Dear playfully.

"Let's say goodbye to your grandson now, Ma'Dear," I say and she reluctantly agrees.

She says a quick goodbye, as I walk up to room no. 1 to say goodbye to Samir. I bid the young man farewell, telling him that I'd be back later tonight. As I leave the room, I notice a queer thing, the space that had held Joshua the giant, was now vacant. Exiting the unit, Wardie reads the question on my ruffled brow and tells me the bare minimum.

"It's been a busy time, and I guess you just noticed, but he has been removed by the parents."

I smile, nod my head, and depart with mother.

"See you later, Wardie," I say.

"See you, Mr. Lawrence," replies the guardian.

"Did you enjoy your time with your grandson Ma'Dear?" I ask as we amble toward the exit.

"Oh yes, it couldn't have been better. I think he knows me," says Ma'Dear gushing a bit.

"Well, ma'am, I would certainly not like to think that all this time spent here talking and singing to him has in any way been wasted," I say with a smile.

Ma'Dear just smiles and nods her head.

I drop her home and head over to the gym for a quick workout. When I hit the gym floor, I immediately notice some girl drama happening near the area where I typically stretch. I catch Ross's, attention and he simply rolls his eyes and continues with his workout. The drama is ablaze, and drawing a crowd so without missing a beat, I head in the opposite direction. I decide to go swim instead because someone would invariably find and regale me with who said what to whom. Swimming laps in the pool usually spares one from that sort of thing.

After about twelve laps, I notice Smitty looking down from the gym, which overlooks the pool. He's signaling that he's headed for the steam room. I squeeze in another five laps and head for the steam room as well. I hear the loud retelling of the drama on the gym floor in full swing. I walk back to the pool and do five more laps before returning to the steam room. Only Smitty remains as I suspected.

"Sup, bruh," says Smitty? "I thought that was you at the door. Where'd you go?"

"Didn't feel like hearing the drama, so I went back for a few more laps," I reply.

"Yeah, leaving me with those knuckleheads," says Will, as we both laugh.

"Those dudes don't understand the concept of a *relaxing steam*. All that drama and loud talk about some bullshit is a complete buzz kill, so I did some more laps," I reply.

"How's the family?" he asks.

When last we spoke was just after Joshua's surgery, so he's reasonably up to date.

"They're good. Loretta is pretty well recovered, and Joshua is gaining weight nicely. I'm headed back there tonight to hang out with him," I report.

"They're going to have to put you on staff soon," jokes Will. "Hey, how about we get a couple of steaks over at Longhorn?"

"Let me give Loretta a call and find out what's happening at home, but that actually sounds great man."

We relax and chat for about ten minutes before hitting the showers. I primp and dress quickly, then head upstairs to wait for Will and call Loretta.

"Hello, ma'am, what's shaking on the home front?" I ask.

"Hey, Donna and Nala are stopping by for a visit," replies Loretta. "Did you get to work out?"

"I got a nice swim, but that was about it I'm afraid."

"Why, what happened?" she asks expectantly.

"There was drama on the workout floor, my dear. There was a loud argument between two well-muscled women that was messing up the workout vibe, so I decided to swim because I just didn't want to hear it or see it," I tell Loretta. "Listen, Will and I are going to get a couple of steaks over at Longhorn. Can I bring you guys anything?" I inquire.

"Maybe a few appetizers," suggests Loretta somewhat tentatively.

"Sounds good, I'll pick out a few nice ones to share among you and your peeps. How does that sound?" I ask her.

"Okay, you and Will enjoy your meal, and tell him I said hello."

"We will, see you in a couple of hours, ma'am," I tell her.

"What'd the lady say?" asks Will, joining me in the waiting area.

"She sends her regards," I tell him. "She's having company and asked me to bring back some appetizers."

The hostess seats us in our accustomed corner and leaves us with our menus.

"I guess this must be our corner," says Will.

"You notice?" I ask. "They always seem to seat us here."

Our server, whom we recognize immediately, comes up and asks to take our drinks and appetizer orders.

"Bloomin' onion," we all say together and laugh loudly.

"How are you, young lady?" asks Will.

"I'm fine, and how are you fellas doing?" asks Willa.

She is a striking young lady with dark hair, dark eyes, and an exquisite Mediterranean complexion.

"I'm fine, fellas. It's good to see you again. Couple of medium well steaks, boys, and a couple of cold ones?"

"We're getting predictable," says Will.

"Okay, next time, we'll shake it up a bit; we'll walk in backwards and sit on the other side of the room. How's that?"

Will howls in laughter as our lovely server shakes her head and smiles wickedly.

Driving home, I glance over at the bag of appetizers on the passenger seat and recall that Will had also taken home some appetizers for his wife. We'll both be heroes tonight, I tell myself, but immediately withdraw the thought. Will is a real life hero who stood tall on the worst day that our city had ever experienced. I do hate when people throw that word around so casually, yet I imagine we're all a little guilty now and then.

Hearing front door open, the three women shout in concert, "Hurry up, we're hungry."

"I'm coming, ladies. I'm going to get you all fixed up in a hurry," I reply.

I walk into the kitchen and greet everyone. Washing my hands, I go for the poultry platter. Seeing the platter, Loretta starts to comment, but I shut it down quickly.

"Come on, honey, you know that I've got to do it properly."

I unpack the appetizers onto the platter, serve the three ladies on the kitchen island, and observe for a moment as they begin to devour the mini-feast.

"Thanks, honey, this is great," says Loretta.

Nala and Donna chime in their appreciation as well.

"You're welcome, ladies," I reply as I disappear into the recesses of the house, closing doors behind me to assure some needed quiet time.

I awaken to the house phone ringing. I roll over in the bed to pick it up, but Loretta has beaten me to it. Checking my phone, I discover that it's past ten o'clock, so I head for the bathroom to wash away the sleep. I find Loretta in the family room with Donna and Nala preparing to leave.

"Ladies, I going over to the NICU to see my son," I tell them as I enter the room.

"Hello, Uncle Von, we were just getting ready to head home ourselves," says Donna.

"Well, ladies, I do hope that you had a pleasant visit," I reply.

"Oh, yes, and the appetizers were right on time. Thanks again," says Nala.

"Don't mention it. The pleasure was all mine," I tell Nala.

"Y'all get home safe, okay?"

"Please give little Joshie our love," says Donna.

"Will do," I reply. "I'll call you later honey," I tell Loretta as I head unto the kitchen to pack up some milk for the little guy.

I place several icepacks atop the milk bottles, seal up the cooler, and head downstairs.

The NICU is eerily quiet this evening as I enter room number four to unpack Joshua's supply of milk. Nurse Lapsingh is busying herself with her notes, but she always acknowledges parents entering the room.

"Good evening, Mr. Lawrence. How are you doing this evening?" she asks, never really looking up from her notes."

"I'm well, Lapsingh, now that I am here," I reply.

"We really have to get some more parents like you in here, Mr. Lawrence," says Lapsingh finally looking up from her work"

"You need to complete a requisition, Lapsingh."

"I'd get a lot of things with a req, but I doubt I'd get that," she says with a wry laugh.

As I walk toward room no. 1, the nurse in charge is eyeing me strangely. As I enter the room, I see why. The corner crib in which the new arrival was ensconced was now empty, which could only mean one thing, our new arrival had passed away. I feel the blood drain from my face, and I feel suddenly cold. I was crestfallen and immediately sought the quite solace of the Parent's Room. I marched in, closing the door behind me, sat down, and burying my face in my hands, cried bitter tears.

This journey, as with any difficult journey, would mean so much more if I could use the gained knowledge to help someone. If I could sit with a family who was at the beginning and pass on some of this experience, it may just be worth it. The tears, just a few at first, eventually came like a torrent, my sobbing prompting Mrs. Coles to come in for a moment to provide a supporting hand on my shoulder. The deluge subsided almost as quickly as it began, and for some inexplicable reason, my thoughts drifted to Yev and his wife.

CHAPTER 17

UNSTOPPABLE

The NICU has, for the past few days, continued to be a very busy place, and Joshua, as if keeping pace with the busy environment, is progressing rapaciously. There are many sick babies coming in daily, and one of Joshua's contemporaries, Raquel, was intubated and has contracted pneumonia. Our prayers are with the family as she has a twin who is also in the NICU.

My little Tai Chi master has actually lost weight this week due to all of his vigorous activity. Young Mr. Wolfe's day nurse nipple fed him to the tune of 5 mls, so the speech therapist that was to have seen him at 11:00 a.m. will have to come tomorrow. Leaving my guy for a few moments, I walk over to fridge to check on his milk supply when the Wardie comes in to report that Joshua has a visitor with whom she is unfamiliar. Walking out to the front with her, I see Rev. Davis, Loretta's *pastor* standing there.

"Hello, Rev. How are things," I ask.

"I am well, Mr. Vonstone. How about you?" replies the parson.

"I have no cause for meaningful complaint," I reply.

"What for, and to whom?" says the reverend in his familiar raspy voice.

"You are so right, sir," I reply.

Loretta will doubtless be pleased that he has come to visit. I take his jacket and usher him over to the sink to wash up. I pass the word to Mrs. Coles that he is Joshua's *pastor* and can have access anytime.

He lingers for a time saying nothing, just standing there with his right hand on the isolette. After about five minutes of silence, he says to me, "There were, as you know, many prayers said for his sake; prayers that would get him here. And now, there are prayers being issued whose purpose is to keep him here."

I smile and look down at my little miracle and remind myself of the story that Loretta told me about a call that she received one Sunday after church.

Loretta would go to church every single Sunday, but as the fertility failures mounted and the injection cocktails took their toll, she would take one Sunday off. Rev. noticed that she'd be absent on the Sunday when newborns were baptized. Rev. told Loretta that she was going about it all wrong. He said, "Be absent on the other Sundays if you want to, but be there in the front row when those babies are brought before God. You need to hold the vision for what you want for yourself, and what better way, than to be down in front being happy for those families."

I don't think that Loretta missed another baptism Sunday while she was able to be out and about.

The Rev. and I bid my son goodnight, and we walk out together. Tomorrow is a really big day, because in addition to being weighing day, I will have the privilege of bathing my son for the very first time. I won't even pretend that I won't be making a midnight run back to the hospital, but I will at least get some sleep in between. Maintaining our home and a home life is really important, but being the vital and ever-present link to Joshua and all that happens at the hospital has become equally important.

I awaken to the gentle buzzing of my phone on the night table. The call is coming in as "private," and I pause for a moment to recall anyone that I know with that name. Unable to recall anyone by that name, I disconnect the call with extreme prejudice. The screen on my Nokia does yield some valuable information; it is now 4:45 a.m., and the sleep having left me, I decide that I'll head for the NICU.

Traffic is surprisingly light at the start of the early rush, and I come upon a spot very quickly directly on Hamilton Ave. across from the emergency entrance. The ambulance bays are teeming with activity, and the ER entrance is equally busy.

I make a decision to head for the front entrance of the hospital, and walking along the side of the hospital, I find that entrance surprisingly quiet. I nod at the security guard as I walk by, and he shoots me a tired nod back. Carroll is surprised as I walk in.

"I don't know why I'm surprised when you walk in, Mr. Wolfe," she says.

"Morning, Carroll," I reply cheerfully as I wash my hands. "How is your night going, young lady?"

"Fine, Mr. Wolfe. I'm getting a lot of reading done," she says smiling.

"Quiet, huh?" I say.

"Mmmhmm ...," replies Carroll.

Laughing, I turn and walk down the hall to Joshua's room and am immediately horrified at the vision that greets me. The room is in a deplorable state with trash bins overflowing with NICU activity product. The floors are sticky from spills. Open packages of used materials litter the various stations, I assume due to the fact that the waste bins are filled. I walk out to the front to find Carroll.

"Has anyone been in to clean and clear the trash, Carroll?" I ask.

"I haven't seen anyone, now that you mention it, Mr. Wolfe," replies Carroll.

I return to the Joshua's room and begin to document everything pictorially. The condition of the NICU is particularly shocking due to the fact that the NICU had, not long before, suffered a costly outbreak. Numerous rules and policy changes were implemented in order to ameliorate the conditions that gave rise to the outbreak. I email a couple of pictures to Dr. Gollisano and follow up with a phone call. The doctor is already awake and immediately knows who is calling. I explain the problem and as I'm talking, he opens the attachment.

"Oh my god! Mr. Wolfe, I need you to send these pictures to the patient safety officer and follow up with a phone call," says Dr. Gollisano.

I take down the number and agree to send a couple of the pictures and make the call as soon as I hang up. Gollisano was shocked, but this guy was quietly angry. He thanked me for paying attention to the problem, apologized for the appalling conditions in the NICU this morning, and most importantly, he assured me that the situation would be immediately rectified.

After hanging up, I go back into Joshua's room, and Nurse Lapsingh and one of the other nurses were giggling and looking at me as they overheard portions of the conversation as I walked about the NICU. I smile back at them and tell them that they'll be okay because they're responsible for patient care, not mopping and trash pickup.

"See, he gets it," says Lapsingh to the other nurse. "All we can do is to call someone, which we did, but no one has come."

About twenty minutes later, as I prepared Joshua's next 35 ml syringe of fortified breast milk, I notice a man walk past the door of the room. It's not so much the man, but the manner in which he is attired that gets my attention. The man is clad in pajamas with an overcoat on top. His pajama pants are stuffed into the boots, and his demeanor is righteously unpleasant.

The man reverses course and enters room no. 3, and as he does, the two nurses busy themselves, heads down.

"Don't you know that you supposed to call the maintenance office number if you have a problem?" says the newcomer, voicing his displeasure at being awakened and summoned here at this wee hour?

"Good morning, sir; if there was any breach in the protocol, the fault is mine, but the condition that I found this room in upon my arrival was nothing short of deplorable. I went from room to room and found the conditions in each room to be worse than the previous. I am the one whom awoke the world to get this disgusting condition remedied. By my account, you don't have a lot of time, so you'd better get to cleaning before the safety officer arrives and finds that you've done nothing to address this disgrace since your arrival," I tell him.

"You have to understand ..." he starts to say as I cut him off like a snake.

"The only thing that I need to understand is that you and I go home when we leave here, to our clean comfortable homes, leaving these vulnerable little ones here. So forgive me if I am completely unsympathetic to your *situation*, whatever the hell that is. *Tick tock,* my lad, you'd better gets to cleaning, before the shit-storm that I just spun up finds you standing here without a mop and pail in your hand."

He glares incredulously at me for a moment.

"*Tick tock, man,*" I say pointing at my bare wrist and turning away from him.

The nurses are struggling to contain their laughter, but I'm really not trying to be funny at all; maybe just a little mean though, I think.

It seems scarcely a day that passes where my little man doesn't do something to absolutely floor me. I managed to occupy myself shopping for furnishings for the nursery during most of the day with Loretta. By the time I made it over to the hospital, it was 10:30 p.m.

"Evening, Wardie, how are you this evening, my dear?" I say to the sentinel of the NICU.

"You turned this place upside down this weekend, didn't you Mr. Lawrence," she asks with an elfish grin?

"I do as I must ma'am, I simply do as I must," I tell her.

"Well, we're getting a lot of attention down here now, I can tell you. Gollisano is happy as a pig in shit because of all that has happened," explains Wardie. "Some don't like the attention though, if you know what I mean, Mr. Wolfe."

"Wardie, I know exactly what you mean and could care less. You know that I don't live here, but Joshua does, and it's for him that I advocate, so anyone that has a problem with a clean, well supervised NICU can kiss my ass," I reply most irreverently.

She throws back her head and laughs loudly.

"Good, I like that," replies Wardie.

"Ma'am, I have been around long enough to know that some will like what you do and some will not, so I just have to ground myself with what is proper and let everything else sort itself out, however it will, ma'am," I say as I walk away from her desk.

As if to give weight and meaning to my conversation with the Wardie, some who would normally greet me as I entered the unit, busied themselves with tasks in other areas and didn't look up. Others went out of their way to acknowledge me, and one in particular made it her business to catch my gaze and cast me a knowing nod, which I returned in kind.

Looking upon my son's face, I notice a remarkable thing. It seems that his life sustaining and ever-present CPAP has been removed. Noticing the surprised look on my face, his nurse comes over to give me a report.

"He has been off of the CPAP for about fourteen hours now and appears to be doing excellently," reports the nurse.

"Thank you, nurse," I reply a bit foggily.

In retrospect, I'm almost glad to have been absent for that one because I may have proved a stumbling block to this new stage in my son's development.

Joshua's former roommate in room no. 4, baby Michael, has passed away, after a valiant struggle against the dreaded NEC. We watched him grow weaker and increasingly jaundiced, his tiny features betraying the terrible stress that the disease was placing on him. It was so difficult to watch. His mom was moved to tears one evening as she came in and found me praying over her son. In truth, I prayed for all the little ones in the NICU, especially the ones whom had no visible support. Loretta and I will attend the funeral this Saturday as Joshua's representatives.

CPAP and weight are the two obstacles to any preemie being discharged to home. Joshua is at fifty hours and counting off of the CPAP. In addition, he has gained one hundred and ten grams since his last weigh-in. The net gain in his weight had led to a commensurate increase in his feed to 43 ml(s). I am preparing to bottle feed him a couple of ml(s) by mouth for the very first time. I am so excited because this is a very great step, one that we most associate with babies. As I hold him close to me, I recall the times he received his feeds through the GI tube, and I'd have him suck on my gloved pinky to help stimulate the sucking impulse. Just at that moment, I'm reminded to discuss actual breastfeeding with the speech therapist. It will mean so very much to Loretta to fulfill this most urgent and primordial of motherly needs, the need to hold her baby close and feed him.

Joshua's long run off of the CPAP has come to an end. Shortly after bottling his entire feed, he *petered* out and had to be placed back on the CPAP, not an entirely unexpected outcome. Joshua has seen the mountaintop and made significant strides toward it. He must now temporarily return to basecamp, but he knows the way back up; he knows the way.

The speech therapist has given the okay for nipple feeding to begin. Mother and child are ready for this, I think. I can't wait to share this news with Loretta.

Baby Michael's funeral is this afternoon. It will coincide with the home going of Lenny Gayle, my high school friend's dad. It will be an evening funeral and likely to be an enormous sendoff. Lenny was a pretty big deal in Brooklyn, and his funeral will be a who's who of the Brooklyn social and political scene. I'm gonna miss the old guy. He's been gone for quite a while though, leaving quite a hole to fill.

Dr. Patel has come up with a strategy for getting Joshua back to the mountaintop. Joshua will spend two hours on CPAP, and one hour off for twelve hours, and then we'll switch to one hour on and two off. The plan is sound and Loretta, and I buy in immediately.

"I think that I can see the end of the tunnel here, honey," I tell Loretta.

Looking up at me as she holds her baby boy, she just smiles and nods her agreement. We're having a magical visit, and I step away to allow her time alone with him. His breathing is very strong as he gazes into his mother's eyes. As the off-hour draws to a close, I head motion to Loretta that we should leave. The nurse discretely sidles over and Loretta reluctantly surrenders her precious bundle.

The atmosphere at baby Michael's funeral was quite an unusual and quite unexpected one. I think that this is due to the fact that Michael lived in a NICU and had no contact with the outside world. The heaviness that would have normally hung over such a funeral did not really exist here. No one had the opportunity to spend time with him, to hold him, and stare into his little face for a resemblance to some other relative. Baby Michael only had a connection to his mom and dad, and of course, those on the NICU. Looking at that little coffin, I imagine the little man inside, and remembered his little body, and the pain I saw on his face at the end, and cried.

There was an almost bizarre juxtaposition between the funeral of Baby Michael and that of Lenny Gayle. The baby without a chance at life, cut short at the very beginning, not having had the opportunity to get to know, love, and be loved by a family, make friends or go to prom. Compare that to Lenny, who lived the full life, married, had many children, built a great, successful business, and had many friends of every description. He died surrounded by his children, grandchildren, and great grandchildren. What might little Michael have done in life? Who might he have become? In what ways might that little man have changed our world?

We pay our respects at the repast and head for Ma'Dear and Pop to pick them up for the Lenny Gayle funeral.

"Are you visiting your son tonight?" asks Loretta.

"I'm feeling somewhat drained, emotionally. I think that I'm going to rest tonight and pick this up in the morning," I reply.

"Did I mention that there is an infant CPR class happening on Monday?" I ask.

"Are you going?"

"I've signed up and plan to go," I tell her.

"You know, usually, when we look at the circle of life, life and death affirm the integrity of the circle. Babies are born, old folks die, and life gets lived in between—that's the nature of it, right?"

"That's how it's supposed to happen, I guess," answers Loretta.

"This day just leaves me confused, empty, and wanting to hold on to what I've got," I say holding her hand.

"I've been trying to put a label on what I've been feeling today, and that just about says what I'm feeling. I just wanted to hold my son right now and not let him go," says Loretta putting her head on my shoulder. Dialing Ma'Dear's number, I tell them we're ten minutes away.

The church is, as expected, at capacity and the daughters are greeting attendees as they arrive. I hug each in turn, and when I get to the youngest, she hugs me and introduces me to her attorney. And thus, the scramble for the fortune begins.

CHAPTER 18

VIGOROUS NIPPLE
PUNISHMENT

Twenty hours and counting is the time that Joshua has been off of the CPAP. His overnight nurse, Betsy, felt that he was doing so well that she simply did not put him back on when the time came. Joshua appears to be doing excellently, but I questioned Betsy about possibly putting him back on, after his feeding, but she said, "Let's see what he does first."

Additionally, Nurse Gabby had switched him over to a nasal feeding tube in order to facilitate nippling, so that's that. There is no going back now.

Bathing my son is truly a moving experience. Watching him react to the aquatic environment just never gets old. Joshua loves a warm soothing bath, followed by a foot rub with a little A&D Ointment. It seems to relax him when he is unsettled. I do so love caring for my son and creating that bond that will doubtless last a lifetime. Lapsingh says that a warm bath and/or food will settle down a cranky baby, or adult for that matter.

Ma'Dear has been a blessing to us in ensuring that Loretta has enough to eat while I am out. Even when there is food in the refrigerator, which is almost always the case, Ma'Dear comes in to keep Loretta's company or watch her sleep. I arrive home to find them both watching television in the family room.

"Hello, ladies. How is everyone?" I ask.

"Hello, son," says Ma'Dear.

"Hi, honey. How's my son?"

"Oh, where to begin?" I ask.

"Well, you can tell us all about it over dinner. What do you have to eat?" asks Loretta.

"I've brought shrimp parmesan for dinner. How does that sound?"

"Set us up," says Loretta.

I move into the kitchen to serve dinner.

"I'm in," says Ma'Dear.

"Oh, let me tell you, Joshua has been off of the CPAP for more than twenty-five hours now," I share.

"Really? Wow!" says Loretta!

"Yeah, his nurse thinks that this may be it. She doesn't see him reverting to CPAP because he is so much stronger now," I say encouragingly.

"He looks really, really good without the CPAP over his face," I say looking at Ma'Dear.

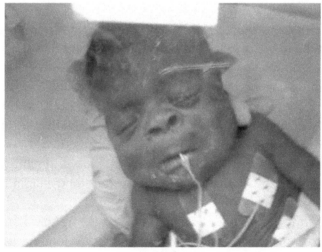

Joshua's face without CPAP

She has her hands clasped together over her chest and appears really happy at the news.

"Did I mention that I've brought dessert?" I ask them.

"No you didn't. Next time, you should lead with that. What did you bring?" asks Loretta knowingly?

"Bread pudding, my dear. I brought bread pudding with that delicious guava sauce. Are there any takers?" I ask.

"Oh, yes, bring it on." she says almost gleefully!

Everyone has roles to play in every endeavor into which we enter. Loretta's role was to carry, nurture, and birth Joshua. My role is that of the utility man. I do what is necessary and what I am asked to do. I manage the intangibles, and these intangibles include waking Loretta in the middle of the night to relieve the pressure on her milk-engorged breasts. Tonight is no exception, and as I gently remove the covers and undo the single button *holding* everything together, she stirs.

"Oh god, this is vigorous nipple punishment," she says.

"I beg your pardon," I reply, unaccustomed to this level of incoherency from Loretta at any time of the day.

"I feel like I'm living in the nipple and bra institution," says Loretta sleepily.

What the hell, I think to myself as I attach the cups and turn on the pump. That was a most peculiar exchange at 4:00 a.m., but not altogether unexpected given the frequent waking. The pump does its work, and in about eleven minutes, there are 8oz of milk ready for the freezer. She was scarcely even conscious during the entire affair with the exception of the strange bit at the beginning.

Joshua has two anomalies at birth that Dr. Gollisano said would be addressed close to discharge. One was a condition called retinopathy of prematurity, and the other a simple hernia. So when Dr. Shah told me that they had scheduled Joshua's surgery, to correct the retinopathy for Monday at 11:00 a.m., we were needless to say, very happy. This obviously meant that Joshua's time in the NICU is drawing to a close, and all of the hopes and prayers of so many people were coming to fruition.

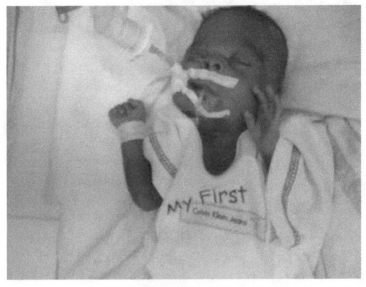

Easter Outfit

Loretta has asked me to lobby for the spinal tap, as opposed to having him intubated again. Loretta has been under anesthesia many times in her life, and I am afraid that the many intubations have affected her voice, so she is keenly aware of what harm can result from intubation. I think that she's worried about his singing voice, if you want to know the truth.

There are rumors circulating concerning the eminency of Joshua's departure from the unit. My boy is 2240 grams today, and that is a mere hairs breath away from the magic number of 2268 grams that will, in addition to the already independent breathing, trigger discharge. Loretta and I are joyful at the prospect of marching him out of Maimonides.

Joshua's retinopathy, originally diagnosed at stage two, had now been observed as having progressed to stage three, which is what made the need for surgery immediate. Loretta wondered out loud if another surgery, with the hernia looming beyond, was really necessary, but I assured her that without it our son's eyesight would deteriorate significantly. She quietly acceded to the necessity of the procedure. Monday morning could not have come any sooner as far as I was concerned. Every step toward discharge was a step in the right direction.

The surgeon, speaking with us in the Parent's Room, assures us that the procedure is quite routine. He assures us that he has performed this selfsame procedure a thousand times, and as if to read my mind, he remarks, "But I know that this is your baby, and nothing is routine."

"Thank you, doctor, you anticipated my very thoughts," I reply as Loretta nods in agreement.

The surgery is as promised, quite uneventful, and relatively quick. It involves a laser cauterization of the periphery of the retina to prevent further decay. The doctor said that he may eventually need glasses and would likely never be a catcher or an umpire, but all in all, we were just fine with that. He has patches over both eyes, but is very much asleep. The patches will come off in about a day or so, but we're not fazed by that. This little boy has been through so much that we've learned to keep the little things in proper perspective.

Mother's Day is looming, and there is an ironic paradox at play this time. Loretta has always held, and quite rightly so, that such recognitions are a bit ridiculous. "People should honor mom and dad every day and not wait for some *special* day to do it. Who knows if mom or dad or any of us will ever reach mother's/father's day?" was her constant refrain. But this time was just a bit different because, for the very first time, she would hold a precious treasure in her arms, who would one day call her mommy. Mother's Day indeed.

Now that almost all the surgeries are behind him, the only remaining obstacle to Joshua's discharge is his ability to nipple his milk (eight feedings daily) and have seven episode free days. The doctors and nurses all say that this is a quite miraculous part of the journey because it always happens quite suddenly. Sometimes, after a difficult day of trying, there'll be a breakthrough, and he/she will spontaneously begin to nipple. I am quite content to wait on *Him*. He came into the world on God's timetable and has spent his time in the unit bathed in *His* grace. He will take his feed compliment in his own good time when he is ready; thanks to *Him*.

Nurse Gabby encouraged Loretta to bring in a special outfit for Joshua for Mother's Day picture taking. Seeing him in his outfit was special in and of itself. Joshua seemed to almost be posing for each picture, but what happened next took us completely by surprise. As if on cue, sensing the gravity of the moment, and knowing that all eyes were on him, Joshua gave his mother the best mother's day present that he could've given her. He began nippling from her breast, eliciting tears from his mom, dad, and Nurse Gabby.

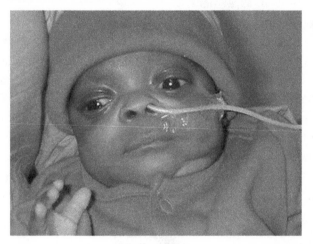

Mother's Day

Dr. Rashdie dropped by Joshua's crib this morning and indicated to me that, on the strength of his weight and his most recent nippling prowess, they were considering discharging Joshua. This came as quite a surprise to me because I was under the impression that Joshua had to nipple all of his feeds for seven days free of episodes before being considered for discharge. I need some clarification so I'll follow up with Dr. Gollisano.

As I anxiously await Joshua's regular weigh-in, I see Nurse Betty come through the door.

"Good morning, Mr. Lawrence. How are you today?" she says cheerfully.

"Good morning, ma'am. Will you be doing the honors this morning?" I ask.

"Yes, I will. Joshua has been gaining nicely, hasn't he?" she comments.

"Yes, I suspect that he may go upstairs into a bassinet soon," says Nurse Betty.

"Como?" I ask.

"That is a step-down room where one nurse monitors a room of children that no longer require critical care," she explains. Graduation, I think to myself. Yes! This is really good news that I can't wait to share with Loretta.

"Hello, mama" I say as Loretta answers the phone.

"Hey, honey. What's new?"

"Well, ma'am, it appears that our son is on the verge of discharge. Can you believe it?" I ask excitedly.

"Are you serious? They're actually talking about it?" she asks.

"Yes, ma'am. I have not yet spoken with Dr. Gollisano, but Dr. Rashdie says that they are moving in that direction," I report. "They may release him as early as next week. He's nippling at 25 mls, is 2340 grams (over the threshold), and has experienced four episode free days."

"Mother is here, and she is very excited that her grand baby will be coming home," says Loretta.

"Hello, son," says Ma'Dear as Loretta hands over the phone.

"Hello, Ma'Dear, your grandson is coming home. How does that sound to you?" I ask her.

"My son, I am more happy than words can express," says Ma'Dear. "Are you coming home soon? I brought some soup for you both."

"Wow, thanks, Ma'Dear. I'll be home soon, okay? Please let me talk to Loretta."

"Hi," says Loretta.

"I'm going to head over to Babies 'R Us to pick up the carrier stroller, okay? I don't think that we can wait any longer," I tell Loretta.

"I agree, let's get on it right away, honey," she replies.

"I'm all over it, honey. I'll talk to you later. Tell Ma'Dear I'll have my soup when I get home."

The news of Joshua's progress just keeps getting better and better. Today, my son has attained 2420 grams. I am assured by the attending nurse practitioner that Joshua will be discharged on Monday if he takes all of his feeds, as he has been, by mouth without episodes. In the words of Dr. Rashdie, "The perfect place in the world for a sick baby is the NICU, and the worst place in the world for a well-baby is the NICU. So all things being equal, if he's doing the things on Monday that he is doing today, we will discharge him."

Will and I get in a quick workout at the gym, and I catch him up on the latest on the discharge watch over a post workout meal. I guess I'll have Ma'Dear's soup for lunch tomorrow.

"So, it sounds like we're getting close, Vonstone," says Will expectantly.

"Man, I am I excited about the prospect," I tell him.

"You've got every right to be excited, man, you're going to have a baby in the house," he says almost mischievously.

"I'm looking forward to it, man. You have no idea how much," I reply.

The New York Strips are a bit tough so we send them back in favor of a few appetizers. We complete our meal in our accustomed chatty laugh fest fashion and part in the parking lot with a promise that we'll check out Madiba, a new South African restaurant Downtown Brooklyn.

Walking back into the house, I find Ma'Dear and Loretta napping on the big brown couch in the family room. I'm not hungry, but I have to have a cup of Ma'Dear's soup. I ladle a cup and pop it into the microwave while I go unpack my gym bag and change.

"How did you slip in without me hearing you?" asks Loretta from the family room.

"You were having a sweet nap, that's how," I reply.

"How is my soup?" asks Ma'Dear?

"I'll let you know in a moment," I reply as I retrieve my soup from the microwave.

"Your soup is delicious, as always, Ma'Dear."

"Thank you, sir," replies the cook. Loretta and Ma'Dear have many questions about the details of the impending discharge.

"All things being equal, Joshua is coming home on Monday," I tell them.

"Is everything ready here at home for my grandson? Is there anything that we need to get? Don't be afraid to let grandma know. I want to do anything that I can."

"We know, Ma'Dear, but I think we have everything covered," I reply.

The weekend is spent in preparation for Joshua's arrival and thinking about Joshua's arrival. We clean out Babies 'R Us of preemie onesies and Pampers Swaddlers, and with that, all preparations for the arrival of the light were complete. As I lay on the floor of his room, looking around at the place that the light will inhabit, tears pour out of a thankful heart.

Monday morning sneaks up on us, and we scarcely can believe that this is the day. Pop calls, and we chitchat until he can contain himself no longer.

"Well, is all in readiness for my grandson's arrival?" says the nervous and expectant grandfather.

"Yes, Pop, everything is ready for the little man. We will leave at ten to get him."

"Coffee's ready," says Loretta from the kitchen.

"Talk to you folks a bit later," I say to pop.

"Call us before you go," he says.

"Okay, Pop," I say patiently.

"What are we eating?" asks Loretta as I walk into the kitchen.

I bend into the warming draw under the stove and retrieve two magnificently prepared omelets, prompting a smile from Loretta.

"Someone's been busy," she says.

"I couldn't sleep," I said smiling sheepishly as we both burst out laughing.

I serve the breakfast on the kitchen island, and we sit and enjoy our omelets, sip our coffee, and talk about the hours that lay ahead.

The hospital entrance is teeming with activity of every description, but as usual, the NICU is an oasis amid all the chaos. I see Dr. Rashdie moving about in the back of room no. 1. Seeing me, he holds up an index finger indicating that he'd be right with us, so we take our baby carrier and head up to the step down room to see our boy. This room was entirely different from the rooms downstairs. It was small, dark, and utterly devoid of a Wardie. It is somewhat difficult to explain the comfort that I derived from knowing that that tough old bird was standing sentinel watch over that NICU. After washing our hands, we find Joshua awake and alert. As soon as Loretta begins to coo to him, he starts kicking his little feet in obvious recognition of his mommy's voice.

"Hello, baby boy, mommy's baby boy. Mommy and daddy are taking you home today," says Loretta. His little feet are churning, as if riding an invisible bicycle.

"I think he heard you, honey." Rashdie finds us standing there with our boy.

"Good news, Mr. and Mrs. Lawrence, I'm going to discharge your son, Joshua, into your care. I just need you to sign some papers, and you may take him home."

Loretta and I look at each other and smile a smile to which only we know the meaning.

And so, it is that with the stroke of a pen at 11:46 a.m. on Thursday, May 16, 2005, and with much joy, adulation, and fanfare, Joshua Olivier Matthias Wolfe, the defacto grandfather of the NICU, was discharged from their care. He was now the whole and sole responsibility of his parents, Loretta and Vonstone. God is great!

There is, however, one final duty to perform. We must do the farewell walk through the NICU, and bid farewell to the NICU staff that is present. Though I know them all, the ones here are not the ones with whom I spent the wee small hours. Opening the door to the NICU, we see Mrs. Coles in her familiar position.

"Mr. Wolfe, I am going to miss you," says the Warden most sincerely. She picks up the phone and announces that Joshua will be taking his final walk out of the NICU.

"I think that this will not be the last time that you see us, Mrs. Coles," I tell her as Loretta and I step to the door into the unit carrying Joshua.

"Oh no," says Loretta, "you have been way too kind to us to let you go like that."

The NICU staff gathers at the door as I hand the carrier to the closest staff as I begin to read.

"Aunties, it is with a grateful heart that I come before you on this day of my discharge. I am grateful for the unbendingly excellent care that allows me to stand in the doorway to the rest of my life. It is with a sad heart that I take this first step, away from all of you toward it. I'm sad because I am leaving my first and constant friends and caregivers. My dad has been my fiercest advocate while I have been here, and may have been a little hard at times, and for that I apologize on his behalf. You have cared for me and made this moment possible, but you both were working together for my highest good. I may not have made it without you both working for me. So, to all my nurses, I say thank you for all that you have done. I promise that my parents will bring me back to visit."

By the time I have finished, the carrier has been passed to the last nurse, and Nurse Gabby hands me the carrier, hugs Loretta, and bids us goodbye at the door.

"Is it me or were some of them crying?" I ask Loretta.

"I saw some tears, but tears or no, they're happy to see you go," replies Loretta as we exit Maimonides for the final time as a family.

"Believe that," I reply laughing.

"That was nice though. I didn't know that you were going to do that."

"Last minute thought. Had to thank them and apologize for the occasional rough edges," I tell Loretta.

"What about the cleaning guy?" Loretta asks mischievously.

"Oh, he can kiss my ass."

Walking away from the hospital with our precious bundle, I half expect someone to say stop, where are you taking Baby Lawrence? That moment passed, however, because upon walking out into the slightly cool May afternoon air, he became forevermore, Joshua Wolfe. We reach the car on 48th Street, and I snap Joshua into the carrier base for the first of many thousands of little car trips. Loretta plants herself beside him and buckles in for the brief ride home.

"I can't believe he's ours," she says looking into his face adoringly.

"I just had the same feeling as we walked out of the hospital."

As we round the corner onto our street, we see a banner draped across the front porch. It read, "Welcome Home Joshua Wolfe, May 16, 2005. Just in case there was any doubt, Joshua was home at last.

All was in readiness inside the house, and I hand the carrier to Loretta inside the front door, and she walked Joshua into his new home where his grandma and granddad were waiting to welcome him.

Loretta held her baby and walked him around the house, introducing him to each and every room.

"Joshua, this is the kitchen, where mommy and daddy cook the food that we eat," she told him.

Ma'Dear and Pop followed behind the tour as it wound its way through the house. I remain in the kitchen to prepare a bottle for my son. When the tour circles back into the kitchen, I ask Loretta if she'd like to try nippling him.

"Oh, by all means," she says. So I prepare the rocker in the nursery with a cloth diaper and a blanket, and she settles in for the first feeding at home.

"I'm going to prep the crib so that you can put him down once he's fed, okay?

"But I just want to hold him," says Loretta smiling and looking at her happily feeding son.

"I'll set the nest just in case you choose to put him down," I tell her.

Ma'Dear has not taken her smiling eyes off of her grandbaby.

"Are you okay, Ma'Dear?" I ask my Mom who is obviously more than okay.

"Your mom has never been more okay in forty-five years," she says smiling sweetly.

"Wow, he's hungry," I remark as I finish with the crib and leave Ma'Dear and Loretta to join Pop in the kitchen.

I pause at the nursery door and observe the scene inside, and the love in there is palpable.

"Can I get you some coffee, Pop?" I ask.

"I feel in a celebratory mood, son."

"We'll make it an Irish coffee then," I tell him with a smile.

"That sounds good, my boy," says Pop laughing.

The evening news is depressing the living hell out of me when the house phone rings.

"Hello?"

"Sup, bruh?" says the voice on the other end?

"Big Willie Style, my boy is home," I report.

"I know. Has the missus put him down yet?"

"Only to go to the bathroom," I tell Will jokingly.

"It's different, isn't it?" asks Will?

"Everything feels different, man. All our thoughts revolve around him and his needs. He's in his crib right now, and Loretta fell asleep in the rocker. I'm going in there and get her into bed as soon as I hang up," I tell him.

"Yeah, and then you're going to take her place in the rocker," says Will as we both laugh.

"Let me know when I can meet the master of the house, okay," asks Will?

"Will do, Mr. Sir. I've got to go now; we'll talk soon."

"Okay, bruh, we'll talk soon," says Will hanging up.

I put the phone on the cradle in the kitchen and walk to the nursery where my family is dozing. Mama is dozing in the rocker, but my son is exhibiting a familiar upper respiratory rattle. In the NICU, his nurse would have applies a drop of saline to each nostril and repositioned, hoping that the saline would soften the mucous and the repositioning would cause him to swallow it. Without waking, Loretta I retrieve a respule of saline and apply two drops to each nostril. Joshua makes the slightest sound and Loretta is awake and looking at me.

"Is everything alright?" asks Loretta, now fully alert.

"He's sounding like he has a lot of upper respiratory mucous," I explain. "I've given him a couple of drops of saline in each nostril, so now, we just wait a few and then turn him to see if he'll express the mucous."

"There's a lot of rattling there. What causes that?" asks Loretta.

"I do not know, my dear. All I know is that he'd get like this under the ideal conditions that the NICU offers, so don't worry, I'll do what they did and we'll hope for a good outcome," I tell her.

"What if we can't deal with this at home, Dr. Wolfe?" asks Loretta.

"That being the case, there's always the hospital, but we're a long way from there yet," I say as I smile and try to assure her.

I turn the little man on his side and prop him there with a blanket. Loretta looks at me, and then at Joshua.

"He sounds worse," she says.

"Not really, the mucous has softened and is moving around a bit more as he is trying to clear his airways," I reply. "I'm going to apply some more saline and prop him on the other side for a bit, which should help as we use the syringe to gently suction his airways."

"You obviously paid attention while our son was in there," says Loretta smiling.

I turned Joshua to the other side and prop him with the blanket. Moving over to the changing table, I extract the syringe and a small plastic bowl from the plastic box where such things are kept. I sterilize them, place the syringe atop a clean cotton diaper, and ask

Loretta to put some warm Nursery Water in the bowl. I am aware that I am being closely watched.

"Now, I am paying close attention. You really know what you're doing," says the mommy as we share a laugh.

"This may be all academic if we wind up in the ER, but let's see what results we get," I reply.

The mucous is really loose now, and I am confident that we'll get most of it out. I lubricate the end of the syringe with some gel, position him and suction the left nostril.

"Pay dirt," I exclaim confidently. I repeat the process with the right nostril, and begin again on the left. The process is quite productive, extracting a significant amount of mucous from both nostrils.

"He sounds so much better," says Loretta as I nod in agreement.

"This calls for a cup of tea, ma'am, and I'm buying."

"Thank you, sir," she says as I turn on the kettle.

We enjoy a lovely cup of tea and chat for a bit about Joshua's doctor appointment tomorrow. I clear the cups to the dishwasher, and Loretta heads for the nursery to move the precious to the bassinette in the master. Loretta calls out to me in the kitchen.

"Honey, come please," she says sounding somewhat alarmed.

From the doorway to the nursery, I perceive the reason for the alarm. The rattling has reemerged, only this time it appears to be deeper in Joshua's respiratory tract. Having been present on occasions too numerous to count when action needed to be taken to clear the airways, I am eminently aware of what needs to happen here.

"I think that he needs to be suctioned," I tell Loretta as she nods in agreement.

"I'll get him ready," she says.

I change quickly, place him in the carrier, and grab the baby bag.

"Nothing more than suctioning is going to happen here. We'll be longer waiting to be seen than actually being seen," I assure her in a gentle voice.

She nods and bids us goodbye with an unavoidably worried look. I shoot her a wink and head down the stairs to the front door with Joshua in tow.

The ER is teeming with unwell humanity of every description. Without hesitation, I bypass the triage window and proceed through the door swung open by a departing client. The now familiar guard looks at me and casts me a familiar nod.

"Hey, man, what's up?" he asks.

Once I explain my situation, he picks up the phone, and asks a triage nurse to meet me on the other side of the inner door to the ER. She's walking over as the door closes behind me. (1:48)

"Evening sir, what do we have here?"

"Well, ma'am, we have a micro-preemie who was discharged today from the NICU upstairs. He has some mucous a bit too deep for a syringe, so I need to have him suctioned," I explain.

She escorts us into an unoccupied room in the triage area and set us up in the examining area. She starts to ask all of the preliminary questions, and I stop her.

"Please allow me to save you some time," I say to her as I retrieve the folder containing Joshua's medical records. She thanks me and disappears from the room. (4:42)

"Mr. Wolfe and Joshua," says the doctor plowing through the door. "I'll need to examine the little fellow before we can proceed."

"But of course, doctor, I understand," I tell the doctor as he approaches, grabbing his stethoscope.

"But first, you'll wash your hands, and sterilize anything that touches my son, yes?"

Without a word, he moves to the sink and washes up, and turning from the sink, he grabs the unsterilized stethoscope and moves toward us.

"You're kidding me, right?" I ask incredulously.

He looks tired and exasperated, but I am resolute.

"Doctor, please allow me to explain. My boy was born at 25 6/7^{ths} weeks, and was released from this hospital only today. Through the care of the good doctors and nurses in the NICU, as well as my vigilance, my boy survived the experience. I know how infection control procedures work, doctor, and I have the number of the hospital administrator here in my phone. So let's get this done right please."

The doctor returns to the sink area and takes a deep breath. He sterilizes the stethoscope and then his hands, before returning to us. (6:36)

"Thank you, doctor, because this is how it must be for the foreseeable future."

He nods and casts me a somewhat snarky smirk. He gives Joshua a good listen back and front before announcing with great confidence *that there are some mucous sounds in there.*

"We'll have to run a few routine tests before we can suction him, though, Mr. Wolfe."

"There won't be any tests run tonight, I'm afraid, doctor. I know how this works because I've been here for three and a half months. The results of any test that you could possibly run can be found in his very recent medical records, of which a copy has already been made. Any still unanswered questions can be answered by calling the NICU and speaking with any attending physician, who will be eminently familiar with Joshua."

"Stand by, Mr. Wolfe," says the doctor, as he stands up and departs the room. (9:11)

"Hey, little man," I say to my son who is wide-awake and looking at me. "I promised you, son, no more poking, prodding, and needles for a while. Daddy is going to make sure that that promise is kept."

He is laughing at the sound of his daddy's voice.

"Hey, what's so funny little boy?" I say tickling his belly a bit.

He laughs even harder. I think about taking him out and holding, but sense that this thing is about to go my way big time, so I resist the temptation. After about ten minutes, the doctor returns with a suction kit, sterilizes his hands, and follows the infection control procedures to a "T."

I really want to say, "Now was that so hard," but I resist. The suctioning is always understandably uncomfortable for Joshua, but it is mercifully brief. He struggles and fusses when the tube is inserted in his left nostril. The tube hits pay dirt early, and begins to extract an ungodly quantity of frothy mucous.

"He should feel much better after this," says the doctor.

"That's the goal," I reply trying to keep the snark to a bare minimum. The doctor finishes up and gives a long listen to Joshua's chest, with the stethoscope, and pronounces him clear as a bell. With that he bids us goodbye and clears us to leave, none too soon, I think. (29:06, total amount of time spent in the emergency room that night) I pack up the folder, grab the carrier, and head for the exit.

"Thanks, man," I tell the guard as we walk by.

"You get him looked at already?" he asks.

"Yes, sir, I did."

"Sheit, that's got to be some kind of record," he says laughing. "You take care of that boy," he says with a knowing familiarity.

"I sure will, and thank you so much, for everything."

The guard smiles a long slow smile, nods, and turns to the client at his station. I reach for my phone to call Loretta, but pause for a moment to breathe the midnight air and look down at my son.

"My precious boy, you're looking to mommy and daddy to make everything aright. We've got you, baby boy. Your mommy and daddy have got you," I say to my son as I dial.

"Hey, I'm on my way home."

"Seriously, you're done, and everything is okay? That was quick, honey."

"Everything is great, and our boy is going to be just fine. I'll see you soon, okay?"

I snap the little fella into the car seat anchor, jump into the car, and take off down Ft. Hamilton Pkwy. As I motor past White Castle, inexplicably, I suddenly have the taste for a tuna sandwich.

EPILOGUE

There are certain events that one expects to occur in particular areas. For example, we expect sand storms to occur in desert areas, hurricanes to churn in the gulf, and tornados to be largely confined to *tornado alley*. In the summer of 2007, the borough of Brooklyn experienced an unprecedented event. In the very early morning hours of August 8, an EF2 spawned somewhere on Staten Island. It proceeded across the *Narrows* into Brooklyn where it ultimately paid a visit to our neighborhood. That morning, I put Joshua into his jogging stroller and went out for a walk. The landscape was surreal with fallen trees, damaged homes and cars, amid blindingly bright sunshine.

On an unusually warm spring evening in 2006, Loretta and I sat in our den on *the big brown couch* watching the evening news. News item after news item featured crimes that were not so much horrific as senseless, and they somehow hit home in an unusual way, after all we are New Yorkers. We looked at each other after each story, and understood that these were the embryonic steps that would culminate in our departure from our beloved vibrant city. In addition, the traffic in the city was getting progressively worse. Getting from place to place was becoming increasingly difficult, and to make things worse, there are plans on the table to put a stadium downtown Brooklyn with no plans for accompanying infrastructure upgrades. Navigating around New York City was really easy years ago. I used to be able to drive into the city on New Year's Eve, or take a slow Saturday afternoon drive up 8th Ave., with the windows down and the music up, through Harlem and over into the Bronx, but now this simple pleasure is no longer much fun.

Loretta attended a holiday event at work where she had occasion to meet with an AVP in her company who worked out of Franklin,

Tennessee. That evening, she told me about this fellow and the conversation that they had. It seems that he was expecting a position to open up in Alpharetta, Georgia, and asked Loretta if she'd be interested. Well, after we talked about the requirements for the position, we decided that she was eminently qualified, perhaps even overqualified for the position.

Discussions began in earnest, after a trip to Franklin, in March to meet with Craig. He offered to fly us down to look over Alpharetta, and the surrounding area, to see if we could live here. We chose the Memorial Day weekend to make the trip, which turned out to be in the high 90s for the entire weekend, but the decision was made; we could live in Georgia, well around Alpharetta anyway. We love Brooklyn, and wouldn't live anywhere else in New York, but we wanted a *different* quality of life for our new son; this was absolutely nonnegotiable. Georgia is a great place for a boy to grow up, and Joshua has flourished here. The biggest challenge for us is exposing him to the diversity of culture so easily accessible in a city like New York, but we manage.

My buddy, Will, with whom I shared so much in New York, and whom I kept in touch with about once every week, died in 2014. He succumbed to a heart attack, brought on by the complications from illnesses acquired while digging in the pile at Ground Zero for the bodies of fallen comrades. I miss him terribly, and am very sad not to have spent more face time with him, or that we never really got the families together. I like to say that I don't have any regrets moving to Georgia, but that would surely be one.

It is always a source of amazement to me how some people are important in our lives at a particular moment, and how central they are to the processes and directions that our lives take. Then for whatever the reason, sometimes none at all, they move to the periphery, and in many cases, they leave our lives altogether. There are some friends whose counsel I value, whose ear I depended on, and whose friendship had great worth to me that are now just irretrievably gone, and that makes me sad.

Ten years have gone by rather quickly. We have enjoyed every minute that we've spent raising Joshua, and wouldn't have done anything differently. I often wonder whatever became of the other

Joshua from room no. 1, how his life evolved, and what he is doing; and for that matter, all of Joshua's neighbors in the NICU.

We've made two trips back to New York as a family. Both trips were in celebration of Joshua's birthdays. The first was at the five-year milestone in 2010, and the second and most recent for his tenth. On each of these trips, we paid a visit to the place where it all started, the NICU at Maimonides Medical Center. It is rare for the staff to be able to see the product of their good work at five years down range; rarer still at ten. It is an expression of our appreciation and esteem for that group of special individuals who lend their time and talents to the care of these the most vulnerable among us, the *preemie*.

Life, my friends, is a journey, a puzzle, a continuum; it is an unbroken line that connects us all, whether we seemingly know each other or not. We are bound together as families, communities, cities, regions, countries, and world. It crosses through into the nether into which our ancestors have passed, and yet binds them to us in ways that I am certain that we cannot understand. On this unbroken line rests truth and falsehood, life and death, the beginning and the end of all things that were, are, and are yet to become. In this continuum, all these exist as mirror images of each other. We cannot know one without knowing the other. One thing does not make sense without being viewed through the lens of the other. What would we know of truth without the lie with which to compare it or righteousness without corruption? Life without end would not be as sweet if not framed by the certainty of death.

Everything in creation that has a beginning, with absolute certainty, has an end. On January 31, 2005, a great light breached the plain of consciousness, joined our reality, and changed everything, forever. The absolute light of our lives turned ten years old on January 31, 2015. So, we ask ourselves, "How can we have an appreciation for the light unless we have journeyed and stumbled through the darkness?" Happy birth year, my precious boy. Your mommy and daddy love you so very much and are so proud of all that you have been, are, and have yet to become.

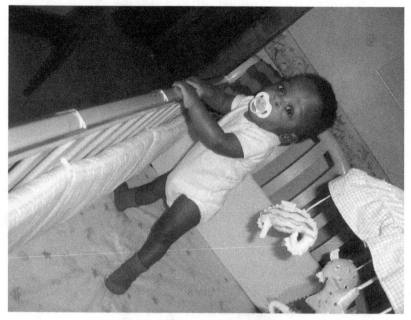

Up and About

Man U

Back to School 2021

In the Band

ABOUT THE AUTHOR

The author, Vonstone Wolfe, is a graduate of CCNY in New York City. He worked, for many years, in various fields of Information Technology in New York. The author and family currently reside in Georgia, but the New York experience entirely informs his experiences.

CPSIA information can be obtained
at www.ICGtesting.com
Printed in the USA
BVHW061136150322
631520BV00001B/70